JIM AND CARMEN NEAFSEY
1260 HOPKINS ST., #2
BERKELEY, CA. 94702

The Church
in the Midst
of Creation

The Church in the Midst of Creation

Vincent J. Donovan

ORBIS BOOKS

Maryknoll, New York 10545

Second Printing, January 1990

The Catholic Foreign Mission Society of America (Maryknoll) recruits and trains people for overseas missionary service. Through Orbis Books, Maryknoll aims to foster the international dialogue that is essential to mission. The books published, however, reflect the opinions of their authors and are not meant to represent the official position of the society.

Copyright © 1989 by Vincent J. Donovan
Published by Orbis Books, Maryknoll, NY 10545
Manufactured in the United States of America
All rights reserved

Manuscript editor: Lisa McGaw

Library of Congress Cataloging-in-Publication Data

Donovan, Vincent J., 1926–
    The church in the midst of creation/Vincent J. Donovan.
        p.   cm.
    Bibliograpy: p.
    Includes index.
    ISBN 0-88344-414-3.—ISBN 0-88344-366-X (pbk.)
    1. Church renewal—Catholic Church.   2. Catholic Church
—Doctrines—History—20th century.   3. Catholic Church—
History—1965–   4. Catholic Church—United States—History—20th
century.   I. Title.
BX1746.D64   1989
282'.09'048—dc19
                                                        88-35614
                                                        CIP

For Bill Schiesl,
who would have understood every line written herein,
and for those I met in his company,
who will, I think, understand the meaning of this book,
because they have lived it

Contents

Preface

To work first in the mission field of the third world and the third church, and then return to and work in the church that sent you to the mission field — the church in America — are two jarringly different experiences. I am not certain which experience provides the greater cultural shock, the journey to a foreign field or the return to the home church. One basic belief serves as common ground between the two experiences: despite the very real differences between the two (differences that sometimes make you question your memory or your sanity), there has to be just one church, one community of Christ. The principles defining the meaning of that church and of its task in the world at last have to be the same, no matter where it is situated. You cannot have two essentially antithetical, contradictory, warring churches and still be able to speak of "one Lord, one faith, one baptism."

What is it like to serve in the third church, which is just coming to be, along with all the agonizing and beautiful revelation contained within it, and then to turn one's gaze — the restless eyes of a missionary — on the second church made up of the diocesan churches of America?

The impressions of that second church are many. An aging church population. The absence of the young in any meaningful numbers. A tired and besieged church; a threatened Catholic school system; a church lacking in sufficient ministers and personnel to reach into the future; a growing number of priests "leading lives of quiet desperation."

And yet a church with lay people, especially religious Sisters, who are more skilled, trained, educated, and qualified than any comparable group in the third church. Lay leadership among men and women with enthusiasm and vision for Christianity that

ix

has to be the envy of every other church in the world. A remarkable, renewed interest in the Bible. Diocesan activities better organized at the chancery level than at any other time in the
life of the church in America as regards youth activity, cate-
chetics, sacramental ministry, and finances—at the very same
time that these identical aspects of church life are dwindling
and heading perilously downhill.

An American episcopacy becoming bolder and more visible
in addressing itself to the moral implications of countless problems of the modern world and national life, yet heading a church
that is highly organized and active at the top, but feeble in the
realistic living out of the Eucharistic and gospel dimensions of
Christian community at the parish level; a church that shows no
reasonable hope of reaching deeply into the twenty-first century
in its present form.

The reflections made in this book are not in narrative or
autobiographical form, but that does not mean they were woven
out of thin air or created in a sterile intellectual laboratory. They
are based on painful personal experience and response to that
experience, present and detectable in every line and between
the lines.

Some of the conclusions developed from Scripture in this
book may be unanticipated, unexpected, and even seemingly
novel and disturbing, but they have been developed with care
and reverence—and with an eye to history. More than one
hundred years ago, Cardinal John Henry Newman, in his "Essay
on the Development of Christian Doctrine," stated that if the
Scripture message is to be understood in an age other than that
in which it was written, in a different place and time, the message has to develop, evolve, and grow in history. Development
and natural growth were contemplated by the Divine Author,
he argues. "The whole Bible is written on the principle of development. As revelation proceeds, it is ever new, yet ever old."
In a memorable passage he opens the door to biblical exploration and discovery: "To the end of our lives and to the end of
the church, the biblical message must remain an unexplored and
unsubdued land, full of concealed wonders and choice treasures.
Of no development of doctrine whatever, which does not actually contradict what has been delivered, can it be asserted that

it is not in Scripture. Everything our Saviour did and said in the New Testament is characterized by simplicity and mystery, which are evidence of revelation, in germ, to be developed; a divine truth subject of investigation and interpretation." Everything Jesus said or did is crying out for development. Are we the only generation in history that is to be deprived of the right of investigation and discovery of those mysteries? Newman's original discovery, which we have not yet fully appreciated or accepted, is the place of history in doctrinal thinking—the true evolution of dogma. We must face the implications of his disturbing thought for our time.

Everywhere I have gone I have heard the same question in one form of another: "We see quite plainly the church as it is, but what *should* it be like?" If you had it in your power to see that church as it ought to be, how would it appear? Not the church in the distant future of science fiction but in the foreseeable, possible future, as we move toward the end of the twentieth century and into the third millennium of Christianity.

It will be a church come of age, under the direction and control of the unpredictable Spirit. It will be a risen church born anew out of the death of the one we now know. The pilgrimage along the road to that church will not be a serene and painless journey. Before we reach the end of that road to a church refounded for our age, there will lie a cross, a crucifixion, not for others but for us.

The time we have already spent on that road has been made up of those missionary moments that we responded to so beautifully, as well as those other moments of stunning possibility, achingly lost forever. We cannot rewrite that history. We trust only that we may learn from it.

The epilogue of this book, of course, never happened—in one place.

The Church in the Midst of Creation

1

Yesterday's Children

The Catholic church of yesterday had a texture to it, a feel:
the smudge of ashes on your forehead on Ash Wednesday, the
cool candle against your throat on St. Blaise's day, the waferlike
sensation on your tongue in Communion. It had a look: the oddly
elegant sight of the silky vestments on the back of the priest as
he went about his mysterious rites facing the sanctuary wall in
the parish church; the monstrance with its solar radial brilliance
surrounding the stark white host of the tabernacle; the indelible
impression of the blue-and-white Virgin and the shocking red
image of the Sacred Heart. It even had a smell, an odor: the
pungent incense, the extinguished candles with their beeswax
aroma floating ceilingward and filling your nostrils, the smell of
olive oil and sacramental balm. It had the taste of fish on Friday
and unleavened bread and hot-cross buns. It had the sound of
unearthly Gregorian chant and *flectamus genua* and mournful
Dies Irae. The church had a way of capturing all your senses,
keeping your senses and your being enthralled.[1]

All this certainly separated us from our Protestant colleagues,
who seemed to distrust all the senses except one, as far as worship of God was concerned. The one sense they trusted was
hearing, and in this they copied faithfully our common ancestors
in the faith, the Jewish people. In their abhorrence of idolatry
the Jewish people believed there was only one way to experience
God and that was to hear him. No statues, no images, no sexual
representations of the deity. You could not see him, touch him,
taste him, smell him. Just hear him and listen to him. "The Lord
has said . . ."; "Hear the word of Yahweh. . . ." A daring poet

1

or artist or psalmist would, on occasion and in seemingly idolatrous fashion, attempt to break out of this biblical straitjacket
with thoughts like, "Taste and see the goodness of the Lord,"
but by and large one avoided such sensual outbursts and remained within the confines of one's religious fears and appre-
hensions, and thus the Jews became the greatest hearers and
listeners in the history of the world. They became people of the
Word, and when they wrote down that Word, people of the
Book.[2]

The classical Protestant Reformers seemed to have inherited
the Jews' perceptions and fears. The Reformed liturgy, performed in stripped-down assembly halls bereft of any dangers
of idolatrous images or representations, consisted in reading the
Word, praying the Word, preaching the Word, singing the
Word—and then considering the worship complete. Catholics
have never been satisfied with this seemingly inchoate liturgy
and have always tried to fill the remainder of their Sunday worship with elements to appeal to all the senses. The body was
made to take part in the worship by standing, sitting, kneeling,
genuflecting, bowing, and striking the breast. And, of course, at
every Catholic liturgy there had to be eating. You could do more
than hear God. You could see God, feel God, smell God, taste
God.[3] This deep involvement of the senses in Christian worship,
often carried out by a church unaware of its profound psycho-
logical and theological significance, has nevertheless left a mark
in the consciousness, in the memory, and sometimes in the long-
ings of the people formed in their values in the times before
Vatican Council II, those people of the past—yesterday's children.

Whatever mixed feelings those people had about the church
of yesterday, doubt was not one of them. There was a sense of
security, an amazing assurance of what they were about. There
was no doubt about confession, the certitude that if they recited
the proper description and number of their sins, they became
as innocent as newborns; that if they fulfilled all the conditions
at Communion time, at the moment of reception, they had on
their tongues and in their stomachs, before the fifteen minutes
of chemical digestion took over, the baby Jesus, or the Good
Shepherd, or the miracle worker of Galilee, or the suffering

Savior, or the risen Lord, depending on the time of the liturgical year. They had no doubt about the power and the glory and the omnipotence and omniscience of those fortunate enough to be among the chosen, ordained priests of the church of God.

There was an assurance about doctrine, so neatly and completely formulated in the Baltimore Catechism. They did not question the central position of the Catholic school as the gem and treasure of the whole Catholic church. It was the "pearl of great price" for which every parish church went out and sold everything it had. The only doubt they had was about the salvation of those young people bold enough and contumacious enough to attend public schools.

And there was no doubt about the bishops, mysteriously and infallibly chosen by the Holy Spirit through a process completely divorced from every political or economic consideration, chosen out of that group of privileged, joyless, nonpastoral, prudent, chancery-trained, businesslike human beings, preordained from all time, born to rule, born to the purple—successors of the apostles.

This system, before Vatican II, was not only accepted but unquestioned—a vast complex of unanalyzed assumptions. Any critique of this system, pro or con, was rare. Elements that could have been encouraged to live and to be fulfilled were left barely understood, such as the five-dimensional approach of the senses in worship as an authentic response to the incarnational basis of the Christian message, and to the sacramental vision of the gospel.

It was necessary to keep that sacramental vision alive—the vision that impels us to see beyond the signs and symbols to the reality toward which they all point, to the Creator behind the creatures of beeswax and incense and ointments, to the whole spiritual world they signify and to which they lead us: the presence of God and God's Christ in the world beyond the shining host. It was necessary because in that very same pre-Vatican II time our culture was insisting to us that there was nothing beyond what we see and hear and smell and touch, nothing beyond what is perceived through the sense organs; that the only true reality is sensory, empirical, secular, this-worldly. Pitirim Sorokin has pointed out that we were in the midst of what he calls the Sensate age, where the only reality was what we could see and feel and measure and count.[4] We needed that sacramental vision to keep the spiritual side of us from being destroyed.

And as for those other elements—that assurance, that being satisfied and no longer searching and questioning and doubting, that unchallenged structure of the church and its ministry that we considered as sacred and unchanging as the gospel—we needed prophecy in the midst of all that, to see what should live and what should die in order to give birth to new forms able to enshrine old values.

We should have asked some hard questions about the parochial schools: whether or not they had become a too willing and subservient ally of business and industry and commerce—and segregation; whether or not they were leading the church away from its task of prophecy. We should have prophesied against the excessive concern for money and goods and things and consumerism that was drowning our world and our church.

We should have prophesied against the colonialism that was crippling our world. Instead, we of the church became part of it. The whole modern missionary movement was born out of colonialism and became part of the colonial structure that was so necessary to industry with its needs for raw materials and world markets. It is no coincidence that the prime example of a modern missionary was David Livingstone, who was from England, the greatest colonial power on earth and the prime instigator of the industrial revolution. Missionary theology was profoundly influenced by colonialism, with missions set up as foreign colonies and the gospel considered a European export. The church should have prophesied, but it remained a silent church.

Finances continued to mesmerize the church. It was difficult to find traces of the New Testament community of Jesus in a modern institution that continued to judge the suitability of its pastors, episcopal and otherwise, on the basis of their financial, administrative, and building abilities. There were financial needs in the original community of Jesus of Nazareth, but they did not constitute the top priority of that community. Judas Iscariot, with his whining shrewdness and manipulative skills, was the one assigned to look after those needs. But he could hardly be considered the model for the church community of our day. At least, one would hope not.

But why should we begin to question and analyze this system now? Is this the time to ask questions about the sacraments, the ministry, the priesthood, the church? Why is this time so special? Perhaps we are attributing too much importance to the time in which we live. Are we making too much of our age? Just because the church is having problems getting men to enter the seminary? Or because so many priests and nuns and brothers are leaving? Or because church attendance has dropped to a scandalous low in the Western world? Because the young in increasing numbers are having nothing to do with the church? Because the last few remaining years of the twentieth century are dwindling away? Because the church is in the midst of a crisis the like of which it has never seen before?

The truth is that for none of these reasons must we look at the church and Christianity in a fresh, new way but, rather, because of something much more profound and disturbing and challenging than any of them.

A THEOLOGICAL LOOK AT OUR TIME IN THE CHURCH

Just when we thought that every possible commentary and explanation of Vatican Council II had already been submitted and digested, Karl Rahner came along and offered an interpretation of the council that was possibly more far-reaching in its implications than anything that had gone before. He was not calling our attention to any particular document that came out of the Vatican Council, or to the intentions of Pope John XXIII in calling the council, or to the conscious plan of the fathers who attended the council. He was interested, not in the interpretation imposed on the council by these figures or by outside agents, but in that interpretation that flowed from the very meaning of the council. He called it a "fundamental theological interpretation of Vatican II."[5]

Sometimes the meaning of important events is not consciously or explicitly intended or even understood by the organizers or agents of those events. Many times during the course of Vatican

Council II there were press conferences set up to explain the meaning and significance of the council in general and of certain documents in particular. It was thought that such conferences and press releases would add importance to the documents or sessions of the council in question, or perhaps even make them important. But when has a press conference or planned fanfare ever inaugurated any great event in history? Or predicted it, or foreseen the tremendous implications of it, or its meaning for history? The meaning of such events is usually seen long after. And so with the Vatican Council. There was no press conference to announce that Vatican Council II was in fact the *church's first official self-actualization as a world church.*[6] That is what Karl Rahner sees as an important fundamental theological interpretation of Vatican II—that the church acted in a real way, for the first time in its two-thousand-year history, as a world church.[7] And we, whether we want to be or not, are now members of a world church—for the first time in *our* history.

This emergence of the church as a world church can be detected in many aspects of Vatican Council II. In the council the church appeared for the first time as a world church in a full official way, as a council with a worldwide episcopate including indigenous bishops from Asia and Africa. In Vatican I the representatives of Asia and Africa were foreign-missionary bishops of European or North American origin. The acceptance of the vernacular in place of Latin as the language for worship was a signal victory for the world church. Latin might be a language of unity for the Western world, but it could never be the language of a *world* church. Only arrogance could make such a claim when 80 percent of the world's peoples speak languages that have nothing to do with Latin. The acceptance of the vernacular was a recognition of the importance of the many cultures of the world, a recognition long in coming to the Roman Catholic Church. The meaning of culture is perhaps one of the most important discoveries of our time, and Vatican Council II aided in that discovery.

The Vatican Council document *Gaudium et Spes* (The Church in the Modern World) begins with one of the most magnificent opening statements a church document has ever had: "The joys and hopes, the fears and anxieties of the people of this age, especially those who are poor or in any way afflicted, are the very same joys and hopes, fears and anxieties of the followers of Christ." If there could be any more striking identification of the mission of the church, of those who call themselves Christians, with the world and the people of the world, where could it be found or what might it be?

For the first time in the church's two-thousand-year doctrinal history, the Vatican Council initiated a truly positive evaluation of the world's great religions, something that had been disastrously lacking until that time and that had made missionary work and missionary dialogue among the people of these religions virtually impossible. The council's statements about the universal salvific will of God, that is, that God truly wills the salvation of all human beings, and that salvation is limited only by the evil decision of human conscience *and nothing else*, throw forever into the trash bin of history the narrow, paralyzing thoughts that have always swirled around the oft-repeated dictum, "Outside the church, no salvation." The implications are stunning: there is a revelation, and a faith that responds to that revelation, which can lead to salvation *beyond* the Christian Word of revelation — a revelation out there in the world, among Buddhists and Hindus and Muslims and people of traditional religions, for them and for us.

Because of Vatican Council II the church has become conscious of its responsibility for the dawning history of humanity. The council has sensitized the Catholic church to its world responsibility. If we have any political theory at all, it is that responsibility. We have taken a qualitative leap. We are no longer a church of the West. The basic presuppositions for a world mission of the world church are now available for the first time.[8]

Karl Rahner sees in Vatican Council II not only the first self-actualization of the world church, but the beginning of a new age, a new epoch in the history of the church. It is a break with the past, a transition from one historical and theological situation to an entirely new one. He sees that, even though the church is nearly two thousand years old, such a radical break with the past has happened only once before in church history and in Christianity, and that was in the very earliest days of the church, when it changed from Jewish Christianity to Gentile Christianity. He calls the first period, or stage, of church history the

period of Jewish Christianity. The second stage he calls the period of Gentile, Hellenistic, European Christianity. The third
stage, which has just begun, is the period in which the sphere
of the church's life is, in fact, the entire world.[9] The second
stage, the Gentile, European stage, was certainly the longest,
and there are subdivisions in it, but not one division radical
enough or decisive enough to constitute a cultural, historical,
theological break with the past in the way that the Vatican
Council's world church heralds the birth of a new epoch.

If we are indeed at the beginning of a new epoch in church
history, that places us in an essentially and basically different
situation for the understanding and preaching of Christianity,
for the ministry of the church, for the understanding and meaning of the church itself—an understanding as different from that
of the pre-Vatican II church as was that of the Gentile, European church from the Jewish church of the first century. What
theological conviction guided so unerringly and so unhesitatingly
that transition from Jewish Christianity to Gentile Christianity?
If we could isolate and identify that theology, that conviction,
what would happen if we applied that theology to the transition
through which we are living today?

It would be immensely helpful if, now, in the midst of the
crisis in our church, in the midst of the fears about the future,
in the midst of the doubts and divisions and bitterness, we could
look calmly at the early church as it faced its first crisis, a crisis
that almost destroyed it, to see how it acted in that crisis. But
we would not want to look at the early church in a sentimental
or nostalgic way, or in a simply pious and edifying way. It would
be of little use to do so. It will be of value only if we look at it
as openly and honestly as we can, letting the story speak for
itself, as we make our way along the road that leads out from
Jerusalem.

THE BROTHER OF THE LORD

We like to imagine that after Pentecost the apostles burst
forth from Jerusalem across the world. It did not happen in
exactly that way. The Hellenistic deacons were the first ones to
go out from Jerusalem to Samaria and Antioch, and to baptize

the first non-Jew, the eunuch of Queen Candace of Ethiopia. The apostles were told that, after waiting in Jerusalem for the power of the Spirit from on high, they were to go out from Jerusalem and Samaria to the ends of the earth. They did not do so. They stayed in Jerusalem and a church grew up there. They continued to be faithful observers of the law and of worship in the Temple, and a kind of Jewish sect emerged there from. They regarded themselves as being a true Israel, the community of the New Testament. Remarkable is the person selected to lead that church. All the Gospels take great pains to point out that the person to head the church of Christ in the world was Simon bar Jona, called Peter. Two other apostles, the sons of Zebedee, were also chosen by Jesus, as recounted in the Gospel stories, to stand with Peter, to witness with him certain cures as well as the glory of the mountaintop and the agony of the garden. Yet when it came time for someone to be chosen to lead the first and only Christian church in existence, it was not Peter or James or John, or any of the apostles who was chosen. Who emerged as the head of the first local church that came to be? It was James, the brother of the Lord. Did Peter, James, and John voluntarily give up the obvious claims they had to leadership and turn it over to the one who came to be called "James the Just"? The historical Eusebius seems to think so.[10] And Clement of Rome stated that the apostles regarded themselves as being responsible for the universal church and placed local churches in the care of prominent men.[11]

One has to wonder if the apostles made such distinctions between local churches and the universal church when the only church in existence was the church in Jerusalem. It seems that soon the preeminence of James was not restricted to the local church in Jerusalem. When Gentiles began to come into the church and conflicts arose, the Council of Jerusalem was called to settle those conflicts. According to the Acts of the Apostles, after Peter and Paul and Barnabas had spoken at the council, "it was James who spoke." "I rule then," said James, sending out a ruling that was to direct the churches outside Jerusalem. The "I" resonates: "*I* rule, not Peter or James or John, but *I*, the brother of the Lord, rule that the following prescriptions be carried out in Antioch, Syria, and Cilicia . . . " (see Acts 15:19–

23). It looks very much as if the leadership of James extended far beyond the local church of Jerusalem. Despite Eusebius' disclaimer to the contrary, he later quotes Hegesippus as saying, "Those who were called the brothers of the Savior governed the entire church, in virtue of their being relatives of the Lord."[12] I think we have to face the unpalatable fact that after Pentecost the family of Jesus took over the church of Christ.

The successor to James, who was to become the second bishop of Jerusalem, was a man named Simeon, son of Cleopas, also a cousin of the Lord. The first fifteen bishops of Jerusalem were men of pure Hebrew stock. Eusebius calls them bishops of the circumcision. Their reign has been described as the Caliphate of Jerusalem.[13]

It did not, apparently, seem strange to the first Christians that the brother of the Lord should be head of the church of Jerusalem. There was a Semitic tradition of such family succession in religious leadership. When Judas Maccabaeus, the great Jewish freedom fighter, was struck down in battle several centuries before Christ, his brother Jonathan accepted the leadership of the Jewish people, was anointed high priest, and took over the command from his brother, beginning the Maccabaean dynasty. The process was still in effect centuries later when another great Semite, Muhammad, died and was succeeded by his brothers and sons in a caliphate that reaches even until our time.

There are indications in the Gospels that Jesus foresaw this very danger of Semitic succession among his own followers and tried to eliminate it. Never once does he allow anyone to lay claim to closeness to him or discipleship merely on the grounds of a relationship of blood. Three evangelists tell the story of the time Jesus' mother and brothers (James among them?) came to see him to take him home, and sent in a message requesting a visit: "Your mother and brothers and sisters are outside asking for you," Jesus was told. "And Jesus replied, 'Who are my mother and my brothers?' And looking around at those sitting in a circle about him, he said, 'Here are my mother and my brothers. Anyone who does the will of God, that person is my brother and sister and mother' " (Mk. 3:31–35; Mt. 12:46–50; Lk. 8:19–21).

Luke records an incident in which a woman declares the

mother of Jesus blessed for giving birth to him and nursing him. Jesus once again puts aside this biological relationship with him as a basis for blessedness and discipleship: "Yea, rather, more blessed are those who hear the word of God and keep it," he tells the woman (Lk. 11:27–28). I think this caution of Jesus about the basis of relationship with him might explain the apparent harshness he shows to his mother in public, as at the wedding of Cana: "Woman, what is it to me and to thee?"

Who was this James, brother of the Lord? He is obviously not James, son of Zebedee, who was martyred by Herod in A.D. 44 (Acts 12:2). Was he James, son of Alphaeus, one of the twelve apostles mentioned in Matthew 10:3? Early writers in the church and most modern Scripture scholars reject such a notion. It is most probable he was not an apostle at all, not one of those whom Jesus deliberately chose, but simply one of his relatives. Mark, in relating a visit of Jesus to his hometown of Nazareth, shows Jesus being rejected by his fellow townspeople as a prophet because of his very ordinary family origins: "Surely this is the carpenter's son. Is not his mother the woman called Mary, and his brothers James and Joseph and Simon and Jude?" (Mk. 6:1–6).

John, too, mentions the brothers of Jesus, but not in the neutral way that Mark does:

> As the Jewish feast of Passover drew near, his brothers said to him, "Why not leave this place and go to Judea and let your disciples see the works you are doing. If a man wants to be known he does not do things in secret. Since you are doing all this you should let the world see." Not even his brothers, in fact, had faith in him [Jn. 7:1–5].

In this passage, John makes a clear distinction between the disciples of Jesus and his brothers. His brothers, presumably including James, did not believe in him, and were urging Jesus to go to Jerusalem, knowing that Jews of Jerusalem were out to kill him. Strange brothers. Jesus' disdainful answer indicates this lack of faith, and hostility: "The right time for me has not come yet, but any time is the right time for you. The world cannot hate you, but it does hate me, because I give evidence that its ways are evil. Go to the festival yourselves: I am not going . . ." (Jn. 7:6–8).

As Mark ends his description of Jesus' visit to his hometown, he seems to agree with John's appraisal, not only of his fellow townspeople, but of his brothers as well: "Jesus said to them, 'No prophet is without honor except in his native place, among his own kindred, in his own house' " (Mk. 6:4–6). It is difficult to conceive of any of these brothers coming to head the church of Christ in Jerusalem. But several of them did.

The books of the New Testament were written in Greek and are part of the Hellenistic Christianity that came to dominate in the church after A.D. 70. They refer only passingly to the terrible difficulties the church went through when, in its beginnings in a Semitic milieu, it was deeply involved sociologically and culturally in the Jewish world. Christianity belonged to the Jewish world because its founder did. Jesus was born of a Jewish mother, was circumcised on the eighth day, observed the Sabbath, went to worship in the Temple, spoke Hebrew and Aramaic, and used the rabbinical method of teaching.[14] Jesus was a Jew and remained a Jew until his last breath. He was a product of Jewish culture. Every word of ethical or moral counsel he pronounced has a parallel in Jewish writings. The concept of Jesus as son of man, son of David, as Messiah and prophet is completely Jewish in character. The ethic of the love of God that he preached, of the love of neighbor, and even of enemies, his predilection for the poor in spirit — all are Hebrew in essence and have counterparts in Jewish writings, as has been often demonstrated, if not in the Scriptures themselves, then in the books of the Essenes and the Qumran documents. Even the idea of resurrection was prepared for by the stories of Enoch, of Melchizedek, and of Elijah in the Old Testament, and by the expectations of the return from the dead of John the Baptist in the time of Jesus himself.

One did not have to give up one's Jewish religion or culture to become a follower of Christ. In fact, the Jewish apostles saw, in the resurrection of Christ, the "Last Things" proclaimed by the prophets of Israel, and called upon all Jews to recognize this epoch-making event. They continued worshiping daily in the Temple and were in no hurry to leave Jerusalem.

The undisputed head of the Hebrew Christian community was James, brother of the Lord, who, standing with the apostles, was the most important personality in the Christian community at Jerusalem.

There was no difficulty, of course, until converts from the non-Jewish world began to join themselves to the Christian community. Paul of Tarsus became spokesman for the Gentile converts, and James, brother of the Lord, the advocate of the Hebrew Christian community. We should not be wrong in seeing in James the founder of Judeo-Christianity, who as such remained deliberately committed to Judaism, in confrontation with Pauline Christianity. In some of the early Judeo-Christian documents still extant, Paul is seen as the enemy and is even accused of duplicity.[15] A rift grew up between Judeo-Christians led by James and Gentile Christians led by Paul, and it was never closed. From the vantage point of the twentieth century it is somewhat surprising to realize that until A.D. 70 the Judeo-Christian wing of the church was the dominant majority, and Paul, in his lifetime, knew only the isolation and pain of the minority. He was triumphant only posthumously.

In the New Testament, written by Hellenists, we have mainly the record of the Pauline missionary expansion of the church. The Judeo-Christian missionary endeavor was just as spectacular. The Judeo-Christian missionaries preceded or followed Paul everywhere he went—Antioch, Galatia, Corinth, Colossae, even Rome. This is the explanation of the repeated references to conflict in Paul's epistles. From the coasts of Palestine and Syria to Asia Minor and Phrygia; from Greece even to Rome there is evidence of conflict and confrontation of the Pauline mission with the Judeo-Christian mission. So strong was the latter's presence that the Roman historians simply looked on Christianity as a Jewish sect. And it is possible that Paul may have become a fatal victim of the Judeo-Christians' enmity in Rome.[16]

When we consider the history of the early church we tend to overlook the tremendous presence and activity of the Jewish Christians who were the first members of the church, and so we miss the extent of the struggle and crisis in the church at the time of Paul. Evidence seems to suggest that the missionary effort that brought Christianity to Africa was Judeo-Christian. When Paul complains that there is no more missionary work to be done (Rom. 15:19, 22, 23), he is curiously silent about missionary work to a place that was to become an important part of the church—Egypt. One thing is certain: Egypt lay outside the field of Paul's mission.[17] Someone else must have evangelized Egypt.

Paul recognized the importance of James in the Judeo-Christian community. In justifying his own apostolate, he mentions that when he went to Jerusalem (A.D. 41) he met with Peter and James, the brother of the Lord (Gal. 1:18–19), and that James, Peter, and John, "these leaders, these pillars of the church," shook hands with Barnabas and himself as a sign of partnership—Paul and Barnabas to work among Gentiles, James and the others among the circumcised (Gal. 2:9–10).

But there were serious conflicts. Paul writes:

> When Cephas came to Antioch, however, I opposed him to his face, since he was manifestly in the wrong. His custom had been to eat with the pagans, but after certain friends of James arrived, he stopped doing this and kept away from them altogether for fear of the group that insisted on circumcision. . . . When I saw they were not respecting the true meaning of the Good News, I said to Cephas in front of everyone, "In spite of being a Jew, you live like the pagans and not like the Jews, so you have no right to make the pagans copy Jewish ways" [Gal. 2:11–14].

The Acts of the Apostles makes reference to this incident and expands on it:

> Some men came down [to Antioch] from Judea [sent by James according to the allusion in Gal. 2:12] and taught the brothers, "Unless you have yourselves circumcised in the tradition of Moses, you cannot be saved." This led to disagreement, and after Paul and Barnabas had had a long argument with these men it was arranged that Paul and

Barnabas and others of the church should go up to Jerusalem and discuss the problem with the apostles and elders [Acts 15:1–2].

In the Council of Jerusalem that ensued, certain members of the Pharisees' party, who had become believers, insisted that the Gentile Christians should be circumcised and instructed to keep the law of Moses. Peter and Barnabas and Paul intervened on behalf of the freedom of non-Jewish Christians. Then James came forth with his famous "I rule then," "and it has been decided by the Holy Spirit and by us" (see Acts 15:19, 28), and agreed that the call of the Gentiles was entirely in keeping with the promises of Scripture. Without mentioning circumcision by name, he stated that non-Jews who accepted Christ should not be burdened by anything except *essentials*. The essentials he listed just happened to be Jewish kosher rules of eating. It is almost certain that, later, Paul ignored these prescriptions as binding on non-Jewish Christians.

For James, to agree that circumcision was not necessary for Gentile Christians was one thing. To agree that it was no longer necessary even for Jewish Christians was something else again. Once, when Paul came to Jerusalem, he went to visit the brothers and, at first, everything went well. Then,

the next day Paul went to visit James, and all the elders were present. He gave a detailed account of all that God had done among the pagans. They gave glory to God when they heard this. "But you see, brother," they said, "how thousands of Jews now have become believers, all of them staunch upholders of the Law, and they have heard that you instruct all Jews living among the pagans to break away from Moses, authorizing them not to circumcise their children or to follow the customary practices. What is to be done? ... Do as we suggest. We have four men here who are under a vow; take these men along and be purified with them and pay all the expenses connected with the shaving of their heads. This will let everyone know there is no truth in the reports they have heard about you and that you still regularly observe the Law" [Acts 21:17–24].

There is James again, broodingly present in the background, agreeing to all the proceedings, letting others speak for him, notifying Paul that they have heard reports about him, reports undoubtedly true, that he is saying circumcision is no longer necessary for salvation even for Jews, and then sending him to perform a strictly Jewish ritual of binding himself to the Temple by a Nazarite vow. This was an extraordinary and even humiliating ordeal to which to subject the apostle of the Gentiles.

The animosity of his Jewish brethren was a distress and agony for Paul until his dying day. He spoke about it often in his letters, and sometimes he felt constrained to burst out in bitter and sorrowful words: "these arch-apostles . . . are they Hebrews? Well, so am I. Are they Israelites? So am I. Are they descendants of Abraham? So am I. Are they servants of Christ? So am I, and even more so than they are" (2 Cor. 11:5, 22–23).

Paul, in his letters, several times praises James, the brother of the Lord. And James, in the Acts of the Apostles, several times mentions that Paul is a man he highly respects and praises for dedicating his life to Jesus Christ. Both James and Paul agree that the saint who has been made holy by grace must show his faith by actually loving, and in this way obeying the law and the commandment of love. But Paul's main interest lies in the meaning of the crucified and risen Christ for those who reside outside the law of Moses, the non-Jews of the world; and James's focus is on the people of the circumcision, his brothers not only in the faith of Jesus but in the faith of Abraham, his brothers in blood and in culture. The differences between these two great and strong men cannot be lightly dismissed, and were in fact never really reconciled. The conflict between them and what they stood for is interwoven with the history of the infant church. But because of their respective writings, we can still catch a glimpse of that painful conflict across the spaces that separated them, across the Christian communities that were divided along with them, across the ages.

PAUL: "No one can be justified in the sight of God by keeping the law" [Rom. 3:20].

JAMES: "But the man who looks steadily at the perfect law of freedom, . . . actively putting it into practice, will be happy in all that he does" [Jas. 1:25].

PAUL: "As we see it, a man is justified by faith and not by doing something the law tells him to do [Rom. 3:28]. We acknowledge that what makes a man righteous is not obedience to the law, but faith in Jesus Christ. . . . We hold that faith in Christ rather than fidelity to the law is what justifies us, and no one can be justified by keeping the law" [Gal. 2:16].

JAMES: "You believe in the one God; that is creditable enough, but the demons have the same belief, and they tremble with fear [Jas. 2:19]. You see now that it is by doing something good, and not only by believing, that a man is justified" [Jas. 2:24].

PAUL: "There is only one God, and he is the one who will justify the circumcised because of their faith and justify the uncircumcised through their faith" [Rom. 3:30].

JAMES: "Take the case, my brother, of someone who has never done a single good act but claims that he has faith. Will that faith save him?" [Jas. 2:14].

PAUL: "If a man has work to show, his wages are not considered a favor but as his due, but when a man has nothing to show except faith in the one who justifies sinners then his faith is considered as justifying him. And David says the same: a man is happy if God considers him righteous, irrespective of good deeds" [Rom. 4:4–6].

JAMES: "This is the way to talk to people of that kind. You say you have faith and I have good deeds. I will prove to you that I have faith by showing you my good deeds. Now you prove to me that you have faith without any good deeds to show [Jas. 2:18]. Faith is like that; if good deeds do not go with it, it is quite dead" [Jas. 2:17].

PAUL: "Has someone put a spell on you, in spite of the plain explanation you have had of the crucifixion of Jesus Christ? Let me ask you one question: Was it because you practiced the law that you received the Spirit, or because you believed what was preached to you? Are you foolish enough to end in outward observances what you began in the Spirit?" [Gal. 3:1–3].

JAMES: "Do you realize, you senseless man, that faith without good deeds is useless. . . . A body dies when it is separated from the spirit, and in the same way faith is dead if it is separated from good deeds" [Jas. 2:26].

If you, the reader, think it is unfair to compare the writings of two men who were not really speaking to each other in their separate letters, then I ask you to look at one final comparison, and make your own judgment on whether they were addressing one another, or not:

PAUL: "Apply this to Abraham, the ancestor from whom we are all descended. If Abraham was justified as a reward for doing something, he would really have had something to boast about, though not in God's sight because Scripture says: *Abraham put his faith in God, and this faith was considered as justifying him*. . . . Think of Abraham again: his faith, we say, was considered as justifying him, but when was this done? When he was already circumcised or before he had been circumcised? It was before he was circumcised, not after; and when he was circumcised later it was only as a sign and guarantee that the faith he had before his circumcision justified him. . . . *This was the faith that was considered as justifying him*" [Rom. 4:1–3, 9–11, 22].

JAMES: "You surely know that Abraham our father was justified by his deed, because he offered his son Isaac on the altar? There you see it: faith and deeds were working together; his faith became perfect by what he did. This is what Scripture really means when it says: 'Abraham put his faith in God, and this was considered as justifying him'; and that is why he was called 'the friend of God'" [Jas. 2:21–23].

JUDEO-CHRISTIANS

The Jewish Christians, led by James, believed in the necessity of circumcision for themselves and, until the Council of Jerusalem, even for Gentile Christians. They believed the Temple was the true place for worship and, like James, they were bound in loyalty to it by a Nazarite vow. They believed the Scriptures were closed and revelation was finished. They felt obligated to the Sabbath, to the laws of Moses and all the kosher rules of eating, and they saw the Gentile Christians as having the same obligations.

The faith of the Jewish Christians was short on doctrine, long on symbols, images, strange esoteric drawings, numbers, secret rites, signs, and angels. Apocalyptic thought is the distinguishing characteristic of Judeo-Christians. They believed in Jesus as the risen One, son of man, son of David, Messiah, and prophet.[18] What they did not come to, and probably could not come to, as Hebrews, was the deepest and fullest meaning of the incarnation and the Trinity.

These Judeo-Christians, who were the dominant force in the original, or Jewish, stage of Christianity, were in a unique position. They had no precedents to follow, since they were the first. The Hellenistic, or Pauline, minority was a nuisance group without power. The Judeo-Christians thought they could convert the world of the pagan Roman empire on their own terms. If any people agreed to join them, let these people, in effect, come to Jerusalem. They were the possessors of the truth and they would dispense it to the world. There was no truth, only darkness, in the Gentile world, and they had nothing to learn from it. There was no revelation waiting for them there. They were reluctant to put their truth, their knowledge of God, their concept of religion, their Christ unconditionally into the hands of the Gentiles. The nations and cultures of the Roman empire were not fit to receive an outpouring of the Holy Spirit, the Spirit of truth, without their mediating it. They saw no reason to look upon those unclean Gentile nations as sacred recipients of God's grace and truth.

Therefore they felt no necessity to reach out to those nations and cultures as equals in the sight of God, no need for searching out, together with those cultures, the meaning of Christ for all of them. In more modern terms, they saw no need for cross-culturation. They were blinded to the fact that they had trapped Christ in their culture.

It must be remembered that we are not talking about the

Jewish people in general, but only about the Jewish Christians of apostolic times. These latter felt that they had a monopoly on the truth. They imagined that they could discover the inexhaustible meaning of Christ for all the peoples of the world from the vantage point of their culture alone. They did not see the absolute necessity of mutual fecundation and interpenetration of their culture with others, toward understanding the meaning of a universal Savior. Christ is the universal Savior only when he is free from the cultural bondage of any one ethnic group. Christ, shackled by the narrowness of one culture, becomes a stumbling block for the Holy Spirit, making the attainment of fuller truth impossible.[19] They did not see how necessary crossculturation was for the understanding of a truth that was universal in its dimensions. They were not ready to undertake the "second exodus" that was required of them. And quite simply, because they made no efforts at cross-culturation, they died. After A.D. 140 there is not a trace of them left in the world of living human beings.

They are not the ones responsible for the transmission of the Christian message in a permanent way to the Roman empire and Europe. It was others who performed the task of leading the church into the second stage of Christianity. The Judeo-Christians stand as a sad and mournful warning to all of us in the church who need such a warning about cultural blindness and arrogance.

It is this first stage of Christianity to which Karl Rahner calls our attention. We can find no other parallel in all church history to which to compare our time. The people of pre-Vatican II formation and instruction are in precisely the same situation as the Jewish Christians of the first age of the church. Those formed in their faith and values before Vatican Council II, that is, yesterday's children, will be tempted to look at the church in the way Jewish Christians did. Yet we, who are yesterday's children, will do so at our own peril, because whether we want to be or not, we are now members of a world church, the sphere of whose life and activity is in fact the entire world.

We can imagine that we are the sole possessors of the truth, that we have a monopoly on the truth, that we have no need of dialogue, no need of mutual fecundation and interpenetration with the non-Christian cultures that surround us, the Hindu, Buddhist, Islamic, traditional-religious, Marxist, scientific-technological cultures that make up our world.

We can pretend that the people of this age do not realize, in an empirical way, in a manner never experienced before by people of any age, that we are indeed adrift in space like all other heavenly bodies, a realization that changes forever our perception of ourselves—as children of the universe, in the midst of creation. We can pretend we do not know that the only possible horizon to give meaning and understanding and evaluation to the Christian message is the planetary horizon of a worldwide experience. We can ignore the fact that Christ will be the universal Savior only when he is free from the cultural bondage of Western Christianity. We can deny that Christ is shackled and trapped in the narrowness of our culture; deny that Western Christ of ours is a stumbling block for the Holy Spirit.

We can refuse to put our Christ and his message into the questionable hands of the anti-Western, anti-Christian people of the world, expecting no revelation from them. We can refuse to enter into dialogue with these people about the meaning of our world, or refuse to be open to conversion if we do. We can refuse to budge from our comfortable view of business as usual in the church, with perhaps a few concessions to the modern world, such as the computerizing of our records and financial figures and communications. We can refuse to admit that we must commit ourselves to an exploration and discovery of a form of the church and its ministry and sacraments, a form of Christianity and of Christ, that we have not known.

We can refuse to do all this, of course, but if we do refuse, we have to ask whether we, the current bearers of the Christian message, will not die and pass from history, just as surely as did the Judeo-Christians, or, later, the African Christians of Augustine's time. They, too, had their day in the sun.

2

The Dying of an Age

THE MIND OF CHRIST

What was the theological conviction that motivated Paul so surely in leading the church from Jewish to Gentile Christianity? There is no doubt about it that Paul fought to free Christianity from its religious and political ties to Judaism. Even though he did not complete the task in his lifetime, he laid the solid foundations for the transition from a Jewish church to a Gentile church. Mainly because of Paul, circumcision was done away with as a requirement for baptism into the community of Christ. Such a step seems obvious to us today. It was hardly obvious or theologically evident in the time of Paul.

The abolition of circumcision for Gentile Christianity, which Paul so fearlessly preached, was not anticipated even by Jesus himself. Since Jesus never preached the gospel to Gentiles in his lifetime, the problem never arose. And you will search through the Gospels in vain for any mention of it. If there had been an oral or written mention of it from the words or deeds of Jesus in the sources of the New Testament, the Hellenistic writers would certainly have made use of it. It could have been argued that Jesus simply took circumcision for granted among all his followers, but Paul considered the acceptance of the gospel by Gentiles a radical break with the past that called for a radically different theological approach. Paul's decisions about circumcision touch not only religion but culture. He is separating the message of Christianity, not only from the Jewish religion, but from the Jewish culture. He is appealing to the gospel message alone as the final criterion by which to judge all responses in faith to that message. At Antioch he felt obliged to remonstrate with Cephas and Barnabas for not eating with Gentiles for fear of the Jews when, in his words, "I saw they were not respecting the true meaning of the Good News" (Gal. 2:14). He believes he is being faithful to the message of Jesus in his own decisions, even if they have to go beyond what Jesus himself anticipated for the practical living out of a life of discipleship. He appeals, in a sense, to the mind of Christ as against the silence of Christ.

How faithful was Paul to the mind of Christ as we can discern it from the pages of the Gospels? Judaism was not only a matter of religion and ethics. It was the sum total of all the needs of a nation placed on a religious basis: economic well-being and prosperity, justice in its courts and rulers, freedom from foreign oppression. Jesus thrust aside all the requirements of national life.[1]

He set up instead an ethical faith system based upon his experience and idea of God. His attitude toward the Roman authorities and to the hated publican tax collectors must have been maddening to his contemporaries. He made no effort to reform the national culture or to eliminate archaic ceremonial or civil laws. He did not come to enlarge the nation's knowledge of art or culture.[2] The truth is, he ignored it. Indeed there is evidence showing that where the prescriptions of this culture clashed with his view of God, he abolished them.

As far as civil justice was concerned, the right of redress and retribution in the courts, Jesus issued a command of nonresistance to violence, theft, and foreign oppression: "turn the other cheek, give up your cloak as well, go the extra mile." In Jewish eyes, such commands led to the end of social order.

The Jews went to great lengths to outline the prescriptions for marriage and divorce in order to regulate and protect family life. Jesus simply prohibited all divorce, and even praised celibacy.

The Jews were noted for their interest in economic development, thrift, diligence in labor — and they had the Bible to back them up. Jesus instead recommends to his hearers the ways of the lilies of the field and the birds of the air, and says to trust in the divine providence of his Father. From the book of Exodus on, the pages of the Bible are filled with laws and rules governing distributive justice to deal with the countless disputes that would arise among the people. Jesus' answer to someone who appealed for his help in acquiring the just share of his inheritance: "Who has made me judge over you?"

The Jews were proud of their system of religious education, carefully nourished over the centuries, and of the products of that educational system—the scribes, the doctors of the law, the Pharisees, the Sadducees and their high priestly caste. On the other hand, there was Jesus with his oft-repeated thought that his message was hidden from the learned and the wise, and was revealed to the little ones, the merest of children. He seemed to have little regard for the religious educational system of the Jews or for the products of that system.

According to a Jewish view of Christ, Jesus' message ignored everything concerned with material civilization and culture. His message is not only not Jewish, but it does not belong to any culture or civilization.[3]

It seems that Paul was indeed respecting and reflecting the mind of Christ. Apparently it was not only national aspirations, the struggle for political freedom, national prosperity, art, music, and culture that Jesus ignored in his preaching. He also ignored circumcision. The true meaning of the Good News, as Paul saw it, had nothing to do with the burden of circumcision. Christ has freed us from that burden.

Paul had a very clear and firm grasp of the Good News. He used it as the criterion against which he measured everything— even the church. Jesus left behind very few prescriptions or regulations about his church. He was no Moses, no Muhammad, no great religious organizer. He left no "church order" or organization, no rituals, no procedure of succession. He clearly established the apostles with authority, but in doing so he was setting up an apostolate, or task, to be carried out, rather than a structure. It is not clear whether he thought there would be need for successors to the apostles before he came again.

Using Paul's method of judging everything by the mind of Christ and the meaning of the gospel, one would have to be very cautious in saying that any offices, or forms of ministry, or types of leadership, or kinds of community, or requirements for membership in the church (besides faith and repentance), or places of worship, or geographical locations, or special days of the week, or rituals for sacraments, were of divine ordinance, or came from the Lord himself.[4] Jesus left the whole thing quite open and free. The choosing of Matthias as replacement for Judas Iscariot, by means of the choice of a short or long straw, is almost comical and could hardly be ascribed to Jesus' directives.

Baptism had been mentioned by Jesus. Circumcision had not. Neither had the Temple as a necessary place of worship. Far from it. The arena of human life, where an offended brother lived, was given preference to the Temple and its worship (Mt. 5:23–24). The prediction of the destruction of the Temple, and the cleansing of the Temple, had contributed to the charges leading to Jesus' death. Jerusalem had not been prescribed as the necessary center for his community. Instead, he had wept over it for its refusal to accept its Messiah, and for not knowing the time of its visitation. The Sabbath and its obligations caused Jesus more than his share of grief. Paul would have all the justification he needed for doing away with a Sabbath that was not "made for man" and superseded human need.

Being very faithful, not to the things that seemed to flow from Jesus' being a Jew or to the interpretations that came from the family of Jesus, but rather to the mind of Christ and to the true meaning of the Good News, Paul felt quite free in doing away, not only with circumcision but with everything that flowed from it, such as the Sabbath and the Temple and Jerusalem itself, as necessary requirements for the church.

Paul did not get involved in the reform of the Jewish church or its renewal. That would have meant countless admonitions and changes of minor things in the conduct of his Christian converts—to lead to a more fervent carrying out of the laws of Judaism. It would have involved, perhaps, making circumcision and its yoke more palatable to Gentile converts, or life as a pseudo-Jew more amiable. For Paul it was time for a clean break from the past, and he did not get trapped in reform or renewal or revitalization of the church. Instead, he lifted matters to an entirely different level. His task was not to reform the Jewish church. It was to enable it to become a Gentile church. Following the mind of Christ and clinging to the heart of the gospel, what Paul did was to *refound* the catholic church, the universal church of Christ.

THE BIRTH PANGS OF A NEW AGE

Karl Rahner, understandably, was interested in the present time as the beginning of a new stage, or epoch, of Christianity, and in the crisis and trauma felt through the length and breadth of the church because of this historical upheaval. There have been others who have seen, in the chaos and pain of our time, not so much just a crisis in the church but, at a much deeper level, a crisis in the world itself, the dying of one age and the birth of a new one. The epicenter of the crisis lies not in the church or in any other institution, but in the world itself. The turmoil felt in the church is merely a reverberation of the revolution that is shaking our world. One of the first persons to put a finger on the death throes of the old age was Pitirim Sorokin, Russian-born philosopher, historian, and sociologist who, in the early 1940s, pointed out that we were caught in a crisis involving almost the whole way of life, thought, and conduct of Western society and civilization.[5] The fact that Karl Rahner showed that the end of an age came to the church in the 1960s is not surprising. It has usually taken the church more than twenty years to notice something happening in the world, and much longer than that to do something about it. The condemnation of slavery, colonialism, racism, antifeminism, and environmental pollution happened in the world long before it took place in the church.

Sorokin has traced history as repeating itself in constantly recurring triple cycles, going back to ancient times, the beginning of recorded history. The first cycle he called the *Ideational* cycle, a time of a unified spiritual system of thought and action, based on a single principle or idea. It is a time marked by a negative attitude or indifference to the sensory world. The first such cycle took place from the eighth century B.C. to the sixth century B.C. throughout the known world, in Brahman India, in Buddhist and Taoist cultures, in Greek and Egyptian societies, in Babylonian and Hindu-Chinese worlds. The literature of the time in all these cultures reflects the almost simplistic, mythological spirit of the age, such as the works of Homer in the Greek culture.[6]

Then in the fifth century B.C. the second cycle began, the *Idealistic* cycle, a time of integrated thought in which reality was seen as partly sensory, partly suprasensory. The major principle involved was synthesis of all thought and life. A good example of this cycle is the Greek culture of classical times, the golden age of Greek philosophy—of Aristotle and Plato. This cycle lasted until the first century A.D., the time when Christ was born.[7]

In the first century A.D. the third cycle began, lasting until the fourth century A.D. This is called, by Sorokin, the *Sensate* cycle, in which true reality is perceived as sensory. Only that is real which we can see, hear, smell, touch, and taste. Reality is empirical, secular, this-worldly. The Roman empire best symbolizes this cycle as the practical, materialistic outcome of Greco-Roman culture. It lasted for the first four centuries of the Christian era.[8]

During these four centuries the seeds of a new age to follow it had already been planted—the seeds of Christianity. And these seeds, once grown to fruitful maturity, brought about a return to the first cycle, the Ideational cycle. From the end of the fourth century, the end of the Roman empire, to the twelfth century A.D., the power of a single idea dominated the Western world. A spiritual, unified system of thought, based on a single principle, took hold. That single idea, that single principle, was God.

God was the fundamental, principal value of medieval culture. And every single aspect of that culture—art, architecture, sculpture, literature, music, philosophy, science, ethics, law, political organization, and family—was formed by that God principle and reflected it. Observers have pointed out that the medieval culture, the history of the Middle Ages, can be described as one gigantic "Amen," one continentwide genuflection to the God of Christianity. During that period, a negative attitude or indifference to wealth and pleasures and to the temporary city of man predominated, an attitude of apparent despising of this earthly life as little more than the testing grounds for eternal life. The "Requiem" might have been the theme song of that Ideational period in history. From the sixth century onward, and as an offshoot of Christianity, the single idea "There is no God but Allah and Muhammad is his prophet" produced in the Arab world what the Christian God effected in the European world.

Then again, in the thirteenth and fourteenth centuries, as the cycle continued to unfold, the Idealistic age returned, when reality was perceived as partly sensory, partly suprasensory, the age of the synthesis of these two perceptions. Thomas Aquinas, master of synthesis, is the ultimate example of this age, of the balance between faith and reason, between Greek philosophy and Christianity.[9]

It seems that each time a particular cycle returns, it comes back in a more intense form than before, more pervasive, more penetrating, reaching more and more aspects of a culture—its effects, in a sense, remarkable. It was certainly true as the fifteenth century dawned and brought with it the beginning of the recurring Sensate age: the sensory, empirical, secular, this-worldly approach that has produced, before running its course in the twentieth century, the scientific-technological breakthroughs that some poets have dreamed of in every age—from flying to hurling themselves at the stars, and unraveling the secrets of the universe in the process.

It is really an age that does not like to conceive of itself as ever ending, but just growing from power to power. And yet, there are seeds already planted in this age that are the beginning of the end of this age, and now point to the birth of a new age. Sorokin sees the signs of the death of this age. "We are at the end," he writes, "of a brilliant 600 year long Sensate day, witnessing the dying of the Sensate culture, and we are at the beginning of a coming Ideational culture of a creative tomorrow."[10] The convulsions going on in our time, so apparent in the 1960s, reveal a crisis that will involve the whole way of life and thought and conduct of Western society and civilization.

Sorokin wrote in the early 1940s, before the atom bomb, before the throwing off of colonialism all over the world, before the civil rights and black power and women's liberation movements, before the hijacking and assassination and terrorism that

have become part of our daily life; before Vatican Council II
and computers and microchips and rockets hurtling toward the
stars; before the fear of nuclear destruction hung like an ever-
present cloud over our planet. The time from the end of World
War II until this writing verifies and exemplifies, with deadly
accuracy, his sober predictions.

And now a return to the Ideational age, Sorokin says, where
a single principle and idea might dominate the epoch coming
upon us; where the suprasensory will be more important than
the sensory, where faith in things we cannot see will be more
important than what we can weigh and measure and see and
feel and count. A single, simple idea. The simple idea or ideology of Marxism? The single, antimodern faith of a simplistic,
fanatical, reinvigorated and purified Islam? The terrible "single
vision" of Bacon and Newton?[11] The final and fundamental substance of the Christian message?

A single, simple idea or principle to dominate an epoch or
an age? In our time? Such a thought might seem possible to
abstract ideologists and philosophers and theologians, but how
could it even be thinkable in the very real, practical, empirical
world of scientists with their complex, ever-growing systems and
disciplines and constantly expanding data? If it is not conceivable in the world of science, however, it is not likely that such
a single, simple concept would have much chance for existence
in the world we know today. But that is precisely the point.
Scientists, too, are part of our world, part of the dying of an age
and the birth of a new one. They, too, are motivated by a vision
of a unified world.

Albert Einstein was driven by the dream of a single, simple
explanation of the entire universe. Of the countless, endless,
sometimes conflicting streams of information coming forth from
the scientific revolution about matter and the universe, he was
convinced that underneath it all was a single principle or idea
that would explain the universe from the smallest particle to the
largest galaxy. That he himself combined the notions of energy
and mass and the speed of light into a single equation was a
stunning step toward the discovery of that principle. He died
without fully attaining his dream and accomplishing that vision.
But there are others today continuing in the quest of that dream,

convinced it is true and authentic. They are in search of a *unified field theory*, a demonstration that the entire cosmos is made up of a few building blocks, perhaps just two particles and a single force. They hope to explain the universe in a single, simple formula that anyone could memorize or jot down on an index card or a T-shirt.[12] The significant factor is that, in this bewildering time in history, people of diverse disciplines, interests, and beliefs, bound together perhaps by a kind of communal need and consciousness, are being drawn by the same powerful and compelling lure of simplicity—the sign of our epoch.

The end of an age in the world and in the church neatly coincide, come together, in our time, in the thinking of both Sorokin and Rahner. Sorokin sees in the new age being born a development of a single spiritual idea or principle, which will form the coming epoch. And what does Rahner see in his vision of a world church developing at the present time? Something very similar to Sorokin.

If the Christian message is to be present in all the world—in Asia, Africa, in the region of Islam and in South America and the Pacific—the manner and matter of proclamation is of paramount importance. How is it to reach the entire world today, this ancient message of Christianity? Using what concepts, what mentality, what ways of thinking, what cultural aspects of understanding and communicating that message? The final, pluralistic form which that proclamation takes will depend primarily on the peoples of the cultures to whom it is proclaimed. But that pluralistic proclamation of the gospel cannot take place until, first of all and *now,* a serious effort is made to take the present versions of the Christian religion and return or reduce them to the "final and fundamental substance of the Christian message." This reduction of the message is a necessary first step toward a new expression of the whole content of faith. From this final and fundamental substance of the Christian message the whole of ecclesial faith will have to be formulated anew along the cultural lines of actual historical situations.[13]

Rahner is calling for, as a necessity for proclamation, a stripping away from Christianity of all the cultural accretions and growths that have attached themselves to it over the ages, all the baggage—a peeling away until we are left with a simple,

supracultural, essential content of the gospel, a salvation event
and its meaning for our world, an idea, a final and fundamental
substance of the Christian message. Is Rahner's description of
the one necessary thing called for by a world church so very
different from Sorokin's depiction of the coming Ideational age?
Or is it, on a spiritual level, very different from what Albert
Einstein dreamed of in the material order?

That single principle, able to dominate the Ideational age,
will be, I believe, more intense, more pervasive, more penetrating, more affecting of all aspects of human life and of all cultures, including the existing scientific culture; more revelatory
of all humankind, of the world and of creation itself, than any
Ideational culture that has preceded it. It is, as Sorokin says,
"the beginning of a creative tomorrow."[14] It will have to be creative, at an intense, personal, communal, faith-filled, and spiritual level. The search for, and identification of, that single
principle or idea on which will be based the unified spiritual
system of thought and action of the world of tomorrow may be
the most important quest of our lifetime, of what is left of today.

A GLOBAL REVOLUTION

If we agree that what we see in the turmoil all around us is
the death throes of the old age and the birth pangs of a new
one, and even admit to the necessity of facing the entire world
in any reflection on the state of the church today, we might still
feel we are floundering hopelessly because we cannot focus practically on what we must do. Rahner and Sorokin and Einstein
are abstract, after all, and do not seem to speak the language
of the people of everyday life with whom we are familiar. If we
truly feel we are called upon to do what Paul did with and for
the people of his generation, to refound the church of Christ,
the whole matter must become more specific, more detailed,
more down to earth, more concrete. It must become as real for
us as the daily newspapers we read or the news programs we
watch on television. Anything else will be so impractical as to
be merely academic exercise.

We have many commentators on our time. One of the outstanding ones, and for our purposes one of the most useful, is

a writer who is a trained observer, accustomed to thorough research, with the skill of a journalist and the keen eyes of a
reporter—Alvin Toffler. Here is what he says about the age that
is upon us: "The dawn of this new civilization is the single most
explosive fact of our time. Humanity faces the deepest social
upheaval and creative restructuring of all time. A global revolution is under way."[15]

Alvin Toffler joins others in seeing in our time the dying of
an age. His divisions of the stages of history differ from those
of Sorokin and Rahner. Rahner, of course, is interested primarily in the church, and his divisions are ecclesiastical and
theological; Sorokin's are cultural and sociological. Toffler's divisions are economic and political. But all these divisions coincide in pinpointing the beginning of a new age in our time:
Sorokin in the 1940s, Toffler in the 1950s, and Rahner in the
1960s.

Toffler conceives of the ages of humankind in waves, the *First
Wave* being the agricultural wave, which held sway from 8000
B.C. to A.D. 1650, when men and women made their living primarily as farmers. The *Second Wave*, from A.D. 1650 to 1955,
was the Industrial Revolution, the era of mass production of
goods. The *Third Wave*, the postindustrial revolution in which
we now live, began, according to Toffler, in 1955, with the use
of the first commercial computer.

Toffler is not interested in Christianity or the church as such,
except insofar as it is one of the institutions affected by the
successive waves of history. We are interested, however, and we
can make use of Toffler's investigations and research in our own
way by focusing on the church in those same periods.

The First Wave, the agricultural revolution, according to Toffler was characterized as the time of the family rooted in one
place, the time of extended families, of many children, of education of the children in the home, of farming communities.[16]

As far as the church in the Western world was concerned,
the parish church was a rural church, and its liturgy reflected
farming life, with rogation days, patron saints of different areas,
and a sense of community in Christian villages. Priests were
trained in rectories and tutored by pastors. The monastic and
mendicant life were ideals.

In the Second Wave, the Industrial Revolution, because of the needs of industry—literacy, obedience, punctuality—schools came into being as an adjunct of industry. They have remained in this questionable alliance to the present day. Education moved out of the homes into the schools. Elderly people, with all their responsibilities and contributions to family and community, were moved out of extended families to homes for the elderly. The mentally deficient were put in asylums. Families became smaller with fewer children, and the nuclear family became the ideal. Families also became mobile, no longer rooted in one place.

During the Industrial Revolution, which almost coincides with Sorokin's most recent Sensate age, there began an excessive concern for money, goods, and things as a by-product and reflection of industrialism. Consumerism was necessary to industrialism. And colonialism became a necessary premise and essential partner to the Industrial Revolution for the procurement of raw materials and as the market for industry's products.[17]

What happened to the church in the time of the Industrial Revolution? The form of the church with which we are familiar was generated almost entirely by the Industrial Revolution. We today have experienced no other form of church. To be sure, there were certain tendencies in the church from the time of James and Paul, and other tendencies that appeared in the second century with the downplaying of the importance of women in the church; and in the fourth and eleventh centuries and other times marked by the proceedings of councils and the proclamations of popes. But these various tendencies were galvanized by the efficiency, power, and success of the Industrial Revolution into a form so rigid that it no longer allows deviation from it, a form of the church considered so sacred and unchanging that it is passed on as being of the same divine origin as its gospel and its founder.

Toffler has done us a service in decoding the principles on which the Industrial Revolution rested and was enabled to function with such stunning success. Once again, Toffler is not interested in the church and scarcely mentions it. But if we take his code and apply it to the church, the results are thought-provoking. The keys to his code—Standardization, Specialization, Centralization, Synchronization, Concentration, and Maximization—when applied to the church are accurate and revealing. They allow the church to stand in a new light, a light that shines on the very human face of the church, and brightens our path enough for us to be able to see clearly—perhaps for the first time, for some of us—what will be involved in the task of "refounding the church of Christ."[18]

3

The Church: Captive of the Industrial Revolution

FROM UNITY TO UNIFORMITY

Unity has always been a goal, indeed a necessity, of Christianity, a need prayed for by Jesus himself: "May they all be one. Father, may they be one in us, as you are in me and I am in you.... May they be one as we are one.... May they be so completely one that the world may believe it was you who sent me" (Jn. 17:21–23).

Paul felt the same necessity: "Make every effort to preserve the unity which has the Spirit as its origin.... There is but one body, one Spirit, ... one hope, ... one Lord, one faith, one baptism, one God and Father of us all" (Eph. 4:1–6). And, of course, there was only one gospel, as Paul took pains to explain to the Galatians: "I am astonished at the promptness with which you have turned away from the one who called you and have decided to follow a different version of the Good News. Not that there can be more than one Good News.... I am only repeating what I told you before: If anyone preaches a version of the Good News different from the one you have already heard, he is to be condemned" (Gal. 1:6–9).

Paul was firm that there could be only one gospel message. It was unchanging and unchangeable. It was a message that came from no single culture, but was meant for all cultures and nations. Surely this is "the final and fundamental substance of the Christian message" to which Karl Rahner refers. Paul

wanted to be certain that the gospel he preached was the same
gospel preached by the other apostles: "Privately I laid before
the leading men the Good News as I proclaim it among pagans.... As a result, these people who are acknowledged as
leaders ... had nothing to add to the Good News as I preach it.
On the contrary, they recognized that ... the same person whose
action had made Peter the apostle of the circumcised had given
me a similar message to the pagans" (Gal. 2:1–8).

Paul had no difficulty concerning the basic message of the
gospel as preached by the other apostles, and they had no difficulty with his basic message. Yet, on the very first step away
from this basic message, diversity arose, and with it, disagree-
ment. The Judeo-Christians felt that, as an authentic cultural
response to that message, they and others had to be circumcised.
The Gentiles, for the very same reasons, felt otherwise. The
Judeo-Christians wanted uniformity in response to the gospel.
Paul fought for the freedom of cultural diversity in response to
the Good News. The battle was joined and in various forms has
continued through the centuries.

An interesting development in the continuing effort to preserve the meaning of the basic message of Christianity came in
the fourth century, in the creation of the Nicene Creed. The
very formulation of the creed by the fathers of the Council of
Nicaea, in the midst of the Greek culture in which they lived,
was a cultural formulation. It had to be. It was an authentic
cultural playing back, as it were, of the original gospel message.
To affirm, as the creed did, that the Second Person of the
Blessed Trinity, the Son, was "consubstantial with the Father,
one in being with the Father," was a thought that the Jews could
probably not have had, and one that today would be culturally
and linguistically impossible for many African and Eastern nations. This leads to the arresting possibility that (1) new light
and even revelation, concerning the meaning and understanding
of the gospel, can come from the cultural situation of those
hearing the gospel (as with the Greeks) and (2) different proclamations of the gospel could constitute historical individuali-
ties, which would be ultimately incommensurable with each
other and with every other proclamation.[1]

Both of these possibilities have tremendous implications for the evangelization of peoples of the third world, and of non-Christian religions. If the Greek fathers could transmit to us further revelation of the meaning of the gospel, so too could peoples of the world not yet evangelized. Peoples of different cultures — both those of the old second church, and those of the new and young third church[2] — can communicate their understanding of the gospel to one another and criticize and enrich one another with this communication. But it has to be admitted and allowed that it might very well be impossible to communicate completely to other cultures the ultimate understanding of the Christian message from the viewpoint of any single culture among them.

People of the old church, the European church, have always claimed this right for themselves — the right of interpreting their own theological pronouncements. But they have not yet allowed the possibility that, because of the "ultimately incommensurable," incommunicable nature of some unique cultural insights and ideas, the peoples of the third church, or of the world not yet evangelized, must be allowed that same right, must be the final judges of their own theological orthodoxy.

Further, if there is room for diversity in the very proclamation and response to the basic message of Christianity, even more freedom has to be called for as we move away from the message to the liturgical, ministerial, sacramental, and organizational carrying out of that message.

That is exactly the way it was understood in the early church. In the second century, liturgical use varied from place to place and from period to period. In the third century, Rome, Alexandria, and Antioch all had well-defined liturgies of their own. At first the language of the church was Aramaic, the language of the church of Jerusalem. Later it became Greek, and finally Latin. In the fourth century, church discipline varied in East and West and from province to province.

Celibacy was not a practice in the Eastern church at all. Nor, during the first three centuries, was there any law of celibacy in the Western church. In the fourth century, different councils, including a council of Rome, passed a law of celibacy for all clergy in the West. It was enforced in some places; in others it was not. All one can say is that the practice of celibacy was spreading. In the fourth century there was a vast array of liturgical forms: Syrian, Alexandrian, Gallican, Roman, Ambrosian, and Spanish.[3]

In the fifth century, as far as the organization of the church was concerned, there were four major ruling patriarchates: Rome, Antioch, Alexandria, and Constantinople, and a few minor ones. Throughout the sixth century there was still no general and enforced law of celibacy. In fact, there were even decrees enacted to regulate the behavior of the wives of clerics. In the seventh century decisive steps were taken to bring about liturgical uniformity, which, in actuality, meant uniformity in the two Western rites—Roman and Gallican. In the eleventh century clerical celibacy was the norm, but local councils still allowed married priests. Celibacy finally became the law in the twelfth century, but in thirteenth-century England priests could still marry.[4]

The people elected bishops in the early church. After that, kings of nations and lords of states and regions exercised that right. Monarchs continued to name bishops until the eighteenth century.

We look in vain for an organized system of training priests during the first centuries of the church. Before the time of Augustine there is no trace of special institutions for the training of the clergy. Instead, young men were attached to the service of a church and assisted a bishop or a priest in the discharge of functions of the church and, by the exercise of duties, gradually learned to look after the church, to read and explain the Holy Scriptures, to prepare catechumens for baptism, and to administer the sacraments. The training to become a priest was personal and practical.

In the fourth century St. Augustine established in his own house a place for clergy to live together. He raised to holy orders those willing to unite community life and the exercise of the ministry. This example was followed elsewhere. For the centuries that followed, young clerics lived in the parish house with parish priests and were instructed by them, or lived in the bishop's house and were instructed there in what came to be known as cathedral schools. Out of these cathedral schools grew the great medieval universities of the thirteenth century. These universities attracted all the illustrious teachers, and the cathedral schools declined. Even so, barely 1 percent of the clergy was able to attend these university courses, which included no practical preparation for ministry. So the vast majority of clergy received no academic training.[5]

The briefest, most cursory glance at church history shows that, although uniformity may have always been a dream of the church, it never was a reality until the Council of Trent in the sixteenth century enabled it to become a reality. At that time a process began, fertilized by the tenor of the times, that led not just to unity and simple uniformity, but to extreme standardization. It did not begin immediately at Trent. After the outbreak of the Protestant Reformation, the need for well-trained clergy was keenly felt. The fathers of the Council of Trent were anxious, for example, to begin a program of proper training for priests, not in itself a call for extreme conformity and uniformity. In the twenty-third session of the council, in 1563, they passed a decree on the foundation of ecclesiastical seminaries. No fixed time of training was legislated, but merely a provision to teach those who were candidates for the priesthood to preach, to conduct worship, and to administer the sacraments. It was much like the training that the early church had provided for its young men — a personal, practical preparation for priestly service while they apprenticed at the side of a parish priest. No prescriptions for theological studies and courses in morality, none for philosophy and church law. All of these came in later, not out of obedience to the decrees of Trent, but because of outside influences that had little to do with the church.[6]

Seminaries were founded in response to Trent's decrees, some immediately, most of them a long time later. A Portuguese seminary was begun in 1564, a Roman seminary in 1565, a German seminary in 1631, and a French one in 1642. It took until the French Revolution to start seminaries in England and Ireland, until 1791 to open the first seminary in America. The beginnings of these seminaries were simple, and a far cry from what seminaries were to become in the midst of the Industrial Revolution that was engulfing the world. Before it was all over, they stood as a fairly good product of that revolution.

We take for granted, today, the standardization of the Catholic church, a process that has become complete in our time. We consider that essential to the church of Christ. Anything less than a standardized church would be unthinkable, heretical, destructive, substantively defective—not only in the minds of the hierarchical leaders of the church, but, alarmingly, even in the view of ordinary priests and lay people. Being members of the Roman Catholic Rite, it has become easy for Catholics to fall into thinking in this manner. It paralyzes the thoughts, freezes one's ideas of the church in a single mold. This paralysis is an obstacle to all missionaries who have ever worked among non-Christian cultures.

Both in non-Christian cultures and in our own, standardized seminaries, priest factories, turned out identical products—standardized priests. The seminaries followed the same course of instructions, with often the same textbooks, in every seminary in the world. There was the same course in dogmatic theology and moral theology, in canon law and liturgy and spirituality, with Scripture, a poor cousin, trailing behind. Not surprisingly, the final products were strikingly similar in whichever part of the world you found them. Their language and thought processes were similar as was their vocabulary. Their spirituality, their idea of what constituted holiness and what militated against it, was painfully standardized. Their notions of prayer were childishly alike. And they were, of course, all male and celibate—a standardized product.

Those who had resisted the standardized molding during the time of training were eliminated along the way—like defective products being pulled off the assembly line. Standardization is supposed to guarantee quality products. It also does away with products that are superior. These priest factories flourished all over the world, especially during the 1960s, with each diocese and religious congregation having its own, but always adhering to the standard. The Industrial Revolution is dying in Western Europe and America, and so are its seminaries. The Industrial Revolution is just reaching the third world, and its seminaries are flourishing.[7]

Religious instructions for children and adults were rigidly standardized before Vatican II, an effect brought about by the issuance of the Catechism of the Council of Trent (1566), and much later, of the Baltimore Catechism (1885). Liturgical rites were completely standardized in the pre-Vatican II church, down to the last word or gesture. Luther's catechisms, large and small, had the same standardizing effect on Lutherans, and the Book of Common Prayer, on the Church of England.

It is noteworthy that the sacraments, not even mentioned as such by name in the New Testament, and floating so freely in the church that they were not defined until the time of Augustine and not put into doctrinal form until the thirteenth century, were finally counted (as was everything during the Industrial Revolution) at the time of the Council of Trent. Seven, no more, no less. That limited number posed no problems for Christians of the Western world, but it did create awkward circumstances for missionaries working in a non-Christian milieu where life and religion were coterminous, and where being born, becoming a woman, growing old, working in the field, and herding cattle were sacred moments — awkward in having to confess that in Christianity there were just *seven* moments of grace or specially Christ-filled occasions — no more, no less.

Not only were the sacraments counted at that time, but their administration became strictly regimented and unchanging. The Mass became severely standardized in the Roman Rite with its one canon, and the fear hanging over it that one word left out in the standardized version of the consecration, or one extra word added, would lead to invalidity, even if that added word were the more correct word or phrase of the Lord's Supper as recounted in the Scriptures. We cannot deny that is where we were; that is the degree to which we were standardized. And, of course, the very language of the church was standardized. It was Latin.

But we cannot blame Trent alone for the state of standardization we have in our church today. Its prescriptions have been used by churchmen of later generations as justification for every manner of control and standardization — an ideal whose roots lie outside the church. After all, we Catholics in America were not raised on the catechism of the Council of Trent, any more than Catholics in other countries were. Lip service was paid to it, and it was used merely as a launching point for catechisms in other languages. We Americans were formed by the Baltimore Catechism, much more rigid and less scripturally inspired than the Catechism of Trent. We have had our own agenda of standardized seminaries and priests and sacraments and celebration of the Eucharist in these latter centuries of the dwindling vitality of the Catholic church, and it has very little to do with the necessity of refounding the church as a true world church.

FROM GENERALIZATION TO SPECIALIZATION

Perhaps the standardization of the church is a coincidence. It just happened at the same time as the Industrial Revolution. Are there any other instances where the two merge? Take the case of *specialization*. We may not be anxious to pursue this matter further because specialization suits many of us very well. And yet specialization is no more an essential mark of the church than standardization. And it has hurt the church no less.

Thomas Aquinas was no specialist. He was a generalist: a philosopher, a theologian, a moralist, a Scripture scholar, a spiritual writer, and a poet. He would have been hard pressed to find a place in the pre-Vatican II church or, indeed, in the church of today. We have witnessed the rise of professionals in the church—the specialists.

In industry, specialization is a necessary component of *standardization*, as parts are designed and put together on the assembly line.[8] It is attention paid to one phase of an operation, and it is work done by part of a person, not the whole person. In our case, specialization is an emphasis on one aspect of the church, or of Christianity, to the exclusion of all other aspects. It is to see all of Christianity under the aspect of morality alone, or of canon law alone. It is to understand it solely from the point of view of psychology, or sociology, or some other aspect. It is to look at dogmatic theology as quite apart from the pastoral ministry of passing on the gospel as a message of hope to a forlorn world. It is to look at the holiness of priests and religious as entirely separate from the sanctity of married lay men and women.

The standardization of the seminaries was made possible by the service of specialists such as dogmatic theologians, moralists, canon lawyers, Scripture scholars, and spiritual directors. There is an ugly side to this specialization, an exclusivity necessarily inherent in it. It is the restriction of knowledge of any particular work or subject to the specialists trained for it. Others are not to mix in or meddle. The pre-Vatican II episcopacy was dominated by canon lawyers. Others who did not belong to this exclusive club were deemed not really eligible. The episcopacy itself became an example of specialization, with those already belonging to it deciding who could become members of it. These canon-lawyer bishops left an indelible legal stamp on the pre-Vatican II church. The secret letters sent out in a diocese to procure names for the selection of a new auxiliary bishop are filled with questions originating from the current bishop about prospective candidates and hence depict qualities that actually describe the bishop who sent the letters.

Others followed in the bishops' wake, taking over specialized areas of the church: the teachers in the seminary, the liturgists, the church historians, the psychologists, the counselors, the sociologists. The hyphenated priest—and a cottage industry—was born. Very often the great gains made by specialists, with their expertise in certain fields, were overshadowed by their virtual illiteracy in other fields, especially in the area of pastoral ministry—sometimes with devastating results for the faithful. It was Karl Barth who sagely advised, "Those involved in active ministry may not leave theology to others," presumably to the specialists, the theologians.[9]

Certain areas such as spirituality, holiness, Scripture, and prayer became the private domain of the specialists, leading people to forget one of the main tenets of the Good News: holiness and the Word of God and prayer are for everyone, not for religious specialists alone.

In an open admission of their debt to, and imitation of, industry, specialists of renewal in the post-Vatican II church boldly transpose the very methods used in business revitalization to the reform of diocesan structures and religious congregations, in everything from mission and objectives and goals to professional burn-out.

Whether we look at the church before Vatican Council II or after it, we have to admit that it has become as specialized as any industry.

FROM LOCAL COMMUNITY
TO CENTRAL HEADQUARTERS

Of all the aspects of the Industrial Revolution that were mirrored in the church, none came into existence so forcefully and unmistakably as *centralization*. Looking back on it now from our vantage point of the late twentieth century, it would almost seem as if the church were always centralized, as it is now. But such was hardly the case. The diversity of liturgies in the early centuries pointed to a diversity of decisions on major matters, made at local levels. The widespread acceptance of such diversity would argue for an early beginning of such diversity, going back to the apostles themselves. The differences in discipline in such things as celibacy point in the same direction. Paul seems to intimate this: "I personally am free. I am an apostle and I have seen Jesus our Lord.... Have we not every right to eat and drink? And the right to take a Christian wife around with us, like all the other apostles and the brothers of the Lord and Cephas?" (1 Cor. 9:1–5).[10]

The existence of different patriarchates shows a sharing of authority in the actual ruling of the church. The fact that the people themselves appointed bishops, and were succeeded in this task by monarchs and rulers of nations (including Napoleon) until the eighteenth century, speaks loudly to the reality of highly independent local churches. Extremely important decisions and policies were being formed at many local levels. Certain bishops were accustomed to running missionary districts overseas.[11] And none of this goes counter to the Gospels, in which Christ is recorded as passing on detailed and special powers to each of the apostles, and not just to Peter. Paul describes all the apostles as having special and unique power in the church (1 Cor. 9:1–5; 2 Cor. 3:2; Mt. 18:18; Jn. 20:23).[12]

At the height of the Industrial Revolution, central control became of paramount importance not only to the industrialists, but also to the near-paranoid church of pre-Vatican II times. The church of the nineteenth century saw itself beset on every side with destructive forces ranged against it: nationalism everywhere, and Italian nationalism uncomfortably close to home;

rationalism, communism, socialism, liberalism, Americanism, and the hostility of an exploding scientific revolution. Pius IX, a "prisoner of the Vatican," appealed to Catholics all over the world for loyalty to the Church of Rome. He used the purely honorary title of Monsignor (invented by the popes during their exile in Avignon) to bind important priests in all the dioceses of the world with a special bond of loyalty and gratitude. They became members of the papal household and were reminded of it in their letters of appointment. Today the office of monsignor is as irrelevant as the notion that the pope is any longer a prisoner of the Vatican.

But from that time on, orders going out to the church, responsible decisions affecting the whole church, could come from only one headquarters, or there would be no control, only chaos. And the nineteenth century, which began with just a few dozen bishops in the world being named by Rome, ended with bishops being appointed by the pope alone.

Priests were to come under the control of the pope through the bishops, even in such matters as the distribution of the sacraments and other pastoral ministry. Priests could not even preach or forgive sins, powers ordinarily associated with ordination, without official approval of the bishop of the diocese where the priest was residing or visiting. And when they did have permission, or faculties, to forgive sins, forgiveness of certain sins was *reserved* to the bishop or even to the pope. Confirmation in any parish was the bishop's exclusive domain. Ordination had to be referred to Rome or to other high church authorities. Even matrimony could not be performed at the parish level, as would seem natural, but had to be channeled in a complex process through the bishop for approval.

Parishes were hopelessly chained to the diocese, and the bishop of the diocese just as inextricably bound to Rome. All the real property in a diocese belonged to the bishop by law, and could not be sold or repaired in a major way without permission of the bishop. The sale of some church property had to be approved by Rome. No one questioned such things, how the ministry of the gospel could have become so irreversibly bound to a human-made structure that the very fact of centralization should be considered as sacred and unchangeable as the gospel.

The drive for centralization was so intense that bishops could not be happy with different departments, such as liturgy or social works or youth ministry or Catholic education, scattered over the diocese. They could not be satisfied until all the heads of the departments of the diocese were gathered together under the bishop's wing, in a single chancery building under one roof — preferably a skyscraper, a tower of power — in the heart of a city. Then every decision of any importance would pass finally through the bishop's office in a smoothly running display of the efficiency of the machinery of church government. No automobile factory could run more effectively.

Communications in the diocese were centralized as well. The bishop himself was the publisher and controller of the Catholic newspaper. The idea of lay people publishing, editing, and controlling Catholic news was unthinkable. And from every department in the chancery an endless stream of documents poured forth, not to serve and assist initiative coming from the parishes, but to direct and control it.

The priest in the parish was at the end of the line in this process, having no other choice but to mirror it in his ministry, with all serious decisions concerning the living out of the New Testament reality in the midst of human life coming from the rectory alone. Centralization was an accomplished fact — and total.

SYNCHRONIZATION, CONCENTRATION, AND MAXIMIZATION

The leisurely, rural way of listing Christmas Masses in the old missals — at night, at dawn, during the day — did not fit in with the time-mesmerized and schedule-dominated atmosphere of the modern pre-Vatican II church. It had to give way to the "Masses on the hour, every hour, upstairs and downstairs"; to the clearing of the parking lot and the six-minute sermon, especially during the 1950s and 1960s when the churches were bursting with worshipers. It paralleled the work-shifts of the factories. Designated hours for confession and baptism, and office hours at the rectory, were taken for granted. What other way could there be? Conversion, forgiveness, and spiritual emergencies had to go by the clock just like everything else. To avail yourself of the ministry of the church, you had to have a watch or you might miss it. Fasting and abstinence were regulated strictly by the clock down to the very minute, as well as the fast before Communion (until the latter was eliminated). The linking of the clock and the church was never really challenged. *Synchronization* was "natural."

The era of the gathering together of multitudes of workers in assembly plants also saw the rise of huge government prisons and asylums and schools, and witnessed, too, the *concentration* of many people in one place for worship. From the sixteenth century onward, we experienced a new type of ecclesiastical architecture: big, factorylike churches to bring the people together in one place at one time.[13] Concentration of many people in one place of worship is more efficient. It serves more people. But it pulls people out of their natural neighborhoods in which they are going to have to live out their Christianity, and it gathers them together in such density that there is no hope of ever finding in its midst the experience of community.

Bigness had become important, too, in the time of the Industrial Revolution. *Maximization.* St. Peter's was the biggest church in the world, and blatantly advertised as such: several football-field-lengths long and wide and high, with the approximate lengths of other famous big churches in the world dutifully marked on the floor in its gigantic aisles. Big parishes, big schools, big dioceses. The importance of a person's ecclesiastical rank depended in large part on the size of one's parish or diocese, with several dioceses jockeying back and forth in their claims for primacy. Numbers became all-important. Numbers of communicants and penitents and marriages determined the vitality of a parish. The amount of money taken in Sunday collections spoke of the status of a parish. Counting all these things and writing them down was of paramount importance in the welter of businesslike administration, accountant mentality, and bookkeeping by double entry that became the job description of a successful pastor—working his way up to a *bigger* parish.

Standardization, specialization, centralization, synchronization, concentration, and maximization. The code of the Industrial Revolution. The end of our own.

4

The Mediterranean Christ

EARLY CONCEPTS OF CHRIST

Reflecting on the church in a dying age, and about the hope of refounding the church for a future age, we have to think about, and consider, Jesus of Nazareth. Christians are, after all, not adherents of a doctrine or members of an organization. They are followers of a person. The knowledge we have of Christ we received from the church, from the first communities of believers who came into being as a movement responding to the historical reality of the man called Jesus. And the growth and vitality of every age of the church are reflected in what the church thinks about the Christ. The stage and development of the church can almost be measured by its ideas and concepts and images of that Christ. He was the Messiah, son of man, Son of God, for the Jewish church. And that was a far step beyond what he was for the Jews who heard his actual voice and saw him face to face, those who believed in him and those who did not, his disciples and his enemies. Something happened between the time those disciples saw him in his lifetime and the time when they came to call him Lord and Messiah.

The resurrection happened. And it changed everything—the way they thought of him, the way in which they perceived him. He was somehow not the same as he had been before, neither in their minds nor in reality. The Gospels testify to this change in Jesus: "Mary stayed outside near the tomb, weeping . . . and saw two angels. . . . They said, 'Woman, why are you weeping?' 'They have taken my Lord away,' she replied, 'and I don't know

48

where they have put him.' As she said this she turned around and saw Jesus standing there, though she did not recognize him" (Jn. 20:11–15).

The other disciples themselves had difficulty recognizing Jesus after the resurrection. John relates the story of an all-night fishing expedition that saw no catch. "It was light by now and there stood Jesus on the shore, though the disciples did not realize that it was Jesus" (Jn. 21:4).

The disciples on the road to Emmaus likewise experienced the same inability to know him: "That very same day, two of them were on their way to a village called Emmaus . . . and they were talking together about all that had happened. Now as they talked this over, Jesus himself came up and walked by their side; but something prevented them from recognizing him" (Lk. 24:13–16).

What was that something that prevented them from recognizing Jesus? What was different about Jesus? We shall probably never know completely, of course, but some things we can deduce with some certainty. His was a risen body, part of the new creation, no longer limited in space or time or to historical accidentals. Before his death he was a Jew, bound by the limits of his culture in language, art, and knowledge. He spoke Aramaic, Hebrew, and possibly Greek. He knew practically nothing of any other culture or its values. He was male, with all the limitations that implies. It was obvious that Mary Magdalene wanted to keep him just what he had been, present exclusively to her. She clung to him, but he told her not to. After his resurrection he was no longer restricted to one place at one time. He was no longer just a Jew, with the limitations of any single nationality. And he was no longer just a male. He was more than a male. He was a complete human being.

What he was now was Lord and Christ.

Peter explains this new state in his first sermon on Pentecost: "God raised this man Jesus to life, and all of us are witnesses to that. Now raised to the heights by God's right hand, he has received from the Father the Holy Spirit. . . . For this reason the whole house of Israel can be certain that God has made this Jesus whom you crucified both Lord and Christ" (Acts 2:32–33, 36).

It is disturbing at first to hear, as Peter seems to say, that only after the crucifixion, at the resurrection to be precise, did Jesus of Nazareth become Lord and Christ. If this is true, then we can no longer identify completely the Christ and Jesus of Nazareth. The two terms are no longer completely interchangeable. They cannot be identically defined and described. Jesus of Nazareth grew into the Christ, or was made the Christ by God, at his resurrection. And since then the Christ has continued to grow—and grow.

It does not matter that this passage of Acts 2 might be a later stage of theological development. It still remains that "the title of Christ seems to be one that he has won through the resurrection rather than through the Davidic association of the title.... It is significant that Jesus is said to have been *made* the Davidic Messiah, not to have inherited the status by right of birth."[1]

The idea of Jesus as truly Son of God, and not just like other sons of Adam; the belief in Jesus as the Second Person of the Blessed Trinity; the belief in the deepest meaning of the incarnation and the divine personality of Christ—these are not ideas that could possibly have come from the Jewish culture or from Jerusalem. These beliefs were not exported from Jerusalem to the world. They were beliefs that grew out of the pagan soil of the Roman empire. They came from the Holy Spirit that was given to the risen Christ, now working in the world. They were an extension of that truth discovered by Peter and his Jewish colleagues much earlier, and much to their amazement: "While Peter was still speaking the Holy Spirit came down on all the listeners. Jewish believers who had accompanied Peter were all astonished that the gift of the Holy Spirit should be poured out on the pagans too" (Acts 10:44–45).

Thus Christ grew to the length and breadth and depth of the Roman empire, and beyond to the whole of Europe. It was a process, under the guidance of the Holy Spirit, of cross-culturation between the people who first heard the message of Christ, the Jews, and all the cultures of the known world. It was a process of revitalization and growth for all those taking part in it. For those who refused to take part in it—the Judeo-

Christians—it meant death without a trace, as surely and completely as if they had never existed.

The process of the growth of Christ continued. In the words of Schillebeeckx:

> Just as in the letter to the Hebrews Jesus was already the heavenly high priest, for the early Fathers God "who became man in order to make man divine" and give him everlasting life, in Byzantium the "Christus Victor," Pantocrator and Sun God, "Light of Light"; so in the early and high Middle Ages he became the one who makes satisfaction, who has ransomed us, and at the same time the Jesus of the *via crucis* and the Christmas manger. Later on, for Luther, he was one who achieved reconciliation with God in a free and sovereign act that covers our guilt and invites us to rely unconditionally on God's favorable verdict; then came the Christ-mystique of the incarnate word in French spirituality of the seventeenth century. ... The Enlightenment saw in him the prototype of human morality, the basis of true camaraderie. The Romantics felt Jesus to be the model of genuinely human personality.[2]

All of these interpretations of Christ, of course, suffer from the possibility of subjective projections of one's own time, unrelated to any reality in the historical life of Jesus. If the projections, however, do refer to a real facet in Jesus' life, which gives a certain direction to those projections, and which serves as a correction to them, there is legitimate room for these interpretations of Christ.[3]

Christ is essentially a mystery and can never be fully understood, and certainly never completely defined by a word or a concept in any culture. Every age has the right to further exploration and discovery of the meaning of that mystery. Every authentic discovery that adds to that meaning is a further revelation in the understanding of Christ. This process of growth in the understanding of Christ within the context of a single culture (or of a group of cultures coalescing into one, such as the European culture) is a process of inculturation—with the message of Christianity growing to the length and breadth and depth of that culture until the two become so intermingled that they are hardly distinguishable. The observation of Hilaire Belloc, though odious to heralds of the gospel working outside Western Europe, was essentially correct in its historical assessment: "Europe is the Faith, and the Faith is Europe." It would have been more theologically (if not literarily) acceptable if he had said, "Europe is the Christian religion. . . ." That is the state of society that Sorokin described as the Ideational stage of history, where a single spiritual idea dominated and formed every aspect of culture: art, architecture, music, law, ethics, literature, and government.

In the case of Europe the inculturation had to be preceded by some cross-culturation involving the mutual fecundation and interpenetration of many tribal cultures that finally merged into the grand culture of Europe: the Jewish and Hellenic cultures merging with the Roman culture, and then the process continuing with the Gallic, Celtic, Teutonic, Slavic, and other cultures of Europe. The further development of the Christian idea took place within the confines of the common European culture. This was no longer cross-culturation but simply inculturation within that common culture.

The process of cross-culturation seems to have ceased in the fourteenth century, after the great assimilation and synthesis of Greek philosophy and European faith in the works of Aquinas. Development after that took place within that one dominant culture. Western theologians looked for no more revelation, and expected none, from outside the culture. They began to think like the Judeo-Christians of the first century. What possible revelation could there be about the Christ outside the pale of Christendom? The great evangelical reformers of the sixteenth century at first thought there was no need to look outside or reach outside Christendom with any kind of missionary apostolate. After all, the great problem of the time was reform within Christendom, within Europe to be more exact.

The Catholic church still felt the need of missionary outreach to the world outside Europe, but its efforts did not result in any true cross-culturation. It was, rather, a case of imposing a dominant culture—a *superior* culture with the gospel as part of that culture—on the inferior cultures of the world. The gospel, with Christ at the heart of it, was a product for export, not to be tampered with in anyway. There was no serious attempt on the part of the church at cross-culturation, interpenetration, or mutual fecundation with the great non-Christian cultures of the world. There were individual efforts in the Far East to do just this in the sixteenth and later centuries, but the Catholic church would not allow these efforts to continue. Arnold Toynbee wryly observes that without this blindness on the part of the church, China might be a Christian country today and the whole history of the Orient might have been different.

The Protestant reformers saw their mistake in downplaying mission and took to evangelizing with great enthusiasm and vigor. But they were no real improvement on the Catholics in their incredibly naive view of Christendom as the sole criterion for a response to the gospel message.

The growth and development of the Christ grew thinner and fainter until it stopped completely. Christianity and Christendom had completely monopolized Christ. It was the second stage of the church: the Gentile, European stage (according to Rahner). Christ was not the universal Savior because he was in cultural bondage to Western civilization.

Mary Magdalene wanted, at first, to keep the risen Christ in bondage also. Symbolically she clung to him, refusing to let him rise, to return to the Father. "Do not cling to me," Jesus said. "I have not yet ascended to the Father." He had to be allowed to rise and return to the Father, so the Father could send the Spirit, the Spirit of Christ—and Christ could be present to everyone at once, not just to Mary Magdalene.[4]

The Western church, too, has clung to Christ, not wanting Christ to rise and go to the Father so the Spirit of Christ might be poured out on all the world—not just on Europe. We criticize the Judeo-Christians of the first century for being narrow and selfish toward the cultures and nations of the Roman empire. Yet our world today is smaller than the Roman empire. The church should have realized that no single group has a monopoly on Christ or on the truth. We should have respected the people of the great religions of the world as "others who hold truth." It would have been, for us the people of the church, a passage from narrow Catholicity to full Catholicity. It is possible that Christ could have continued to grow if he had been opened to the Hindus, Buddhists, Muslims, and others of the world. They could not have added to what we know of Jesus of Nazareth, but they could have contributed entirely new dimensions to our understanding of Christ—if Christ is indeed the universal Savior.

Christ was not offered in any honest way to them, but was restricted to Europe. And Christ, shackled by the narrowness of the one European culture, became a stumbling block for the Spirit and the world. The restriction of Christ for centuries to Europe almost certainly ensured the stultification of Christ. There was nothing further, nothing new, for Europe to say about Christ. It had said everything it could. All that was left were countless, spiritless repetitions and memorizations of the repetitions.

This was the last part of Rahner's Gentile, European stage of the church. It was also, in Sorokin's description, the Sensate age, when only that was real which could be seen and heard and touched and measured and counted. It was known as the Scientific age as well.

Coming to the end of the line, with nothing further to say, it was inevitable that the European church, this time with Protestant initiative, would turn, not to Christ, about whom it had nothing more to say—and which subject the sciences had no way to measure and count and weigh—but to Jesus of Nazareth, the historical Jesus. With the most modern deductive tools at its command, it began to investigate Jesus of Nazareth scientifically, measuring and analyzing all the data it could find, all the sources it had available and could uncover, concerning him. So began the quest for the Jesus of history.[5]

SEARCHING FOR THE HISTORICAL JESUS

This quest began in the late eighteenth century and blossomed in the nineteenth century, bringing with it a change in the image of Jesus. Using scientific methods of studying original documents and types of literature and distinctive linguistic characteristics, exegetes began to see that the historical Jesus *as he really was* presented a different picture from the one put forth by the Bible and Christian tradition. There was a difference between the historical Jesus and the Christian image of Jesus. It was thought that sheer objective scientific methods would be able to retrieve a purely historical and undogmatized Jesus from the interpretation given to Jesus by people of his own time and every time thereafter, including ours. Such was faith in the so-called exact sciences of the nineteenth century. Unfortunately, the purely objective and exact sciences were not so pure and objective. The historical and critical study undertaken in the quest for Jesus had a clearly antidogmatic and antiecclesiastical bias and purpose behind it.[6]

What kind of purely historical Jesus did that study produce? A Jesus that was a projection of the ideal notions of humanity at that time—an obviously nineteenth-century-European humanity. What a coincidence! Jesus became an empty blackboard, a tabula rasa, on which could be written the evolutionary and utopian dreams of the century. So much for objective, exact science.[7]

The exegetical historians of the time thought so much of their method that they began to identify what could be ascertained by systematic research about Jesus with the Jesus who actually lived; as though the only reality of the actual life of Jesus of Nazareth was what they, nineteen hundred years later, could know by research. They identified *being* (Jesus' actual life) with *being aware of* (what they could scientifically learn about Jesus' life).[8] The 90 percent of his life that they could not retrieve scientifically did not exist.

They did discover, though, that there truly was a great difference between the historical Jesus and the Christ of faith, so they came up with many solutions to this problem. Some (like Rudolf Bultmann) saw no connection between the two—Jesus and the Christ. They actually saw an essential break between Jesus of Nazareth and Christ of the kerygma. The Christ of Christian preaching was all-important. The historical Jesus of Nazareth did not matter. It made no difference what Jesus did or thought. What mattered was the Christ preached for our salvation, and faith in that Christ. It is interesting to note that the Christ who was so important for Bultmann was the Christ of the kerygma, the Christ proclaimed in the New Testament writings, not a Christ who had grown beyond that. It would have been of no interest to Bultmann, nor would it have had any meaning for him, to look for the meaning of the Christ beyond the confines of Europe.[9]

Others (like Käsemann) denied such a radical break between the Jesus of history and the Christ of the kerygma. They relativized the distinction between the two, seeing enough historical validity in the Christ who was preached after the resurrection to link him to the Jesus who actually lived — a connection made by the fellowship Jesus had with his disciples. When these disciples preached the risen Christ, they *remembered* the actual Jesus they had seen and touched and handled, and the belief in the risen Christ brought back to life their memories of Jesus in a different light.[10]

This effort of searching for the historical Jesus has yielded untold benefits for all of us, and the historico-critical method of Scripture study and exegesis, which it engendered, has changed the face of modern theology. Since *Divino Afflante Spiritu*, the papal encyclical freeing Catholic scholars to pursue Scripture studies with honesty and integrity, Catholic exegetes and theologians have joined in the quest for Jesus, and would agree with their Protestant colleagues that the question of absorbing the historico-critical method into Scripture studies and theology is a matter of life or death for Christianity.[11]

At the same time, this obsessive search for the Jesus of Nazareth "that really was" has taken up the energy of most theologians and has left the growth of Christ, and the meaning of Christ for our world, for the most part untouched. Only outside Europe and North America has there been any new and invigorating effort to look at the meaning of Christ in a modern, flesh-and-blood world of today. Liberation theology and black theology (as a countercultural thrust against Western theology) are the exciting and controversial results.[12]

A PLANETARY CHRIST

We have to admit that after all this extensive and scientific scholarship, after nearly two thousand years of Christianity, the Christ that is worshiped in our churches, the Christ that is the basis for our church and all its faith life and activity, is no more than a Mediterranean Christ. That is as far as Christ has grown. European and American theologians see nothing wrong with that, nothing wrong with the fact that we have not even begun to think of, or search for, the meaning of a planetary Christ, a world Christ. We continue to let all our efforts revolve around a Mediterranean Christ. We of the West have monopolized Christ.

Yet the Spirit of Christ is still active everywhere in the world, not just in Europe. The Spirit is still being poured out on non-Christians, as much to our astonishment as it was to our Jewish forebears in the time of Peter and Cornelius. Revelation is still going on in the midst of traditional religions, Hinduism, and Buddhism, in the knowledge behind the scientific revolution, in the universe—in all creation. The universe constitutes the primary revelation of the ultimate mystery from which all things emerge into being; and if we believe Paul the apostle and John the evangelist, Christ is at the heart of that mystery. There is surely more to be revealed about the Christ than is already known. But we, trapped in our own culture with its exact and measured scientific view of the world, with our lack of sacramental vision, may not be the ones to discover it. Like Mary Magdalene, we are afraid to let go of Christ, to let Christ out of our grasp, out of our control.

An interesting dispute broke out some time ago in secular and religious journals about what was termed "the end of Catholicism."[13] A Catholic writer in a secular magazine (*New York Review of Books*) focused on the very thing we have been discussing here—the "scientific exegesis of the New Testament"—and on some of the startling conclusions to which it led: the lack of belief in Jesus' miracles, Jesus' ignorance of his own divinity and of the Trinity, and finally the inability to believe in the resurrection of Christ and eternal life for us. The author claimed that there was a "liberal consensus of Catholic theologians" on all these subjects, and this was the theology being taught in Catholic seminaries today. He maintained that once one accepts the scientific methods of Scripture interpretation, Catholic theology seems to break down, and eventually one comes to the end of Catholicism.

The author of the article was, of course, immediately attacked by a Catholic theologian and a Catholic sociologist writing in a Catholic magazine (*Commonweal*). The Catholic theologian admitted that there is a "liberal consensus" in Catholic thought, but that it is restricted to the historico-critical method of looking for the Jesus of history in the New Testament writings and does not extend beyond that. Beyond that, there is a wide divergence of interpretations in Catholic theology, and there is no such thing as a liberal consensus denying the divinity of Christ, the resurrection, and life after death. The only thing denied is that there is evidence enough in Scripture to come to a definite answer about the mind of Christ—what Christ actually thought about such things. Many things reported as being said by Jesus are really the thoughts of Christian writers put down long after Jesus was gone. They are not the thoughts of Jesus. The theologian claimed that the writer in the secular magazine, while correct in seeing a "liberal consensus" in the acceptance of the historico-critical method of Scripture studies, is wrong in stating there is a consensus among theologians about the church and Christ and Christianity. There is no such consensus. Catholic theology is not breaking down.[14]

The Catholic sociologist took another tack against the critic of Catholic theology, who had also said that there seems to be a necessity of choice between a fundamentalist interpretation of the New Testament and agnosticism (the inability to know anything about God and Christ from the Scriptures). The sociologist argued that the scientific method is not the only valid way of knowing. There is another authentic way of knowing, and that is by *naming*, by using *models* to explain our experience of God and things religious; in this view religion is just one of many cultural systems that are made up of symbols, pictures, models, and stories and that attempt to explain our experience. Religion attempts, by symbols, to explain the ultimate meaning of life. Science merely explains the meaning of observable phenomena. These are two different things, two different cultural systems, and science cannot speak of ultimate realities. And so the critic of Catholic theology is wrong in imagining that the end of faith is in sight simply because the historico-critical method of biblical scholarship turns up no historical proof for the divinity of Christ or the resurrection. Modern theories of knowing provide other ways of coming to true faith.[15]

It is to be noted in this dispute, carried on in the pages of the *New York Review of Books* and *Commonweal* magazine, that the point at issue in the discussion is the scientific analysis and exegesis of the New Testament. It troubles the critic of Catholic theology, even though he admires the skill in the use of it. It is taken for granted and defended by the theologian, who joins his Catholic colleagues in considering its use of utmost importance, a matter of life or death for Christianity. Its danger is put aside by the sociologist, who finds in his own scientific discipline an alternative way of knowing and believing. The sociologist, unlike the other two, at least opens the door to the world outside Europe and America by introducing the notion of cultural systems of symbols and images as an authentic way of coming to the truth. He also cautions against the false hope of science ever speaking of ultimate realities.[16]

One has to wonder to what extent the theologians of this "liberal consensus" of scriptural interpretation have unquestioningly accepted the basic premise of the Scientific, Industrial, Sensate age—that only that which can be seen and touched and weighed and measured is real, and that the only real truth is scientific truth. To refer to the acceptance of the historico-critical method of Scripture study as of life-and-death importance for Christianity seems to bear out that premise and conviction. The fact that the scientific method is completely Western in its bias, and might not be so completely objective as one would like to imagine, is not considered very important.

One could prescind from the arguments, pro and con, about the importance of this method, or the dangers inherent in it, and still come to the same disturbing conclusion as did the original criticism of Catholic theology in the *New York Review of Books*—but for entirely different reasons. Because theology has neglected the question of the further exploration and discovery of the mystery of Christ for the whole world and for our time; because it has confined itself to the sterile, in-turned, seminary-academic world of Europe and America; because it has refused to engage in the process of cross-culturation with the non-Christian cultures of the world; because of its historic inability to dialogue successfully and meaningfully with the whole world of the East and with the modern world of technology—Catholic theology might well have reached the limits of its own language, where it seems to have broken down. It is possible that it has nothing more to say, and we might indeed have come to the end of Catholicism—Western Catholicism. In this age of the world church, it is precisely to that world that we have to turn, to discover life and growth once more for our Mediterranean Christ.

5

Sacraments for the World

NOT IN JERUSALEM

Believe me, woman, the hour is coming when you will worship the Father neither on this mountain nor in Jerusalem. . . . The hour will come—in fact it is here already—when true worshippers will worship the Father in spirit and truth: that is the kind of worshipper the Father wants. God is spirit and those who worship must worship in spirit and truth [Jn. 4:21–24].

We have spoken of the dying of an age and the birth of a new one, and have adverted to the direction in which the signs of the times and the history of the church seem to be pointing us—outward. Outward not only as the direction toward which we must focus in our church activity and ministry, but outward as the arena in which we shall find the meaning of our church and ministry.

The Jewish Temple and the Gentile temple, the mission compound in the foreign fields and the parish church on the home front, the diocesan chancery and the Vatican—all had one thing in common: the belief that all holiness and truth and prophecy came from within; that true worship was effected from within; that the meaning of faith somehow originated from within. There are indications in the Bible and elsewhere that this belief might not be altogether true.

There is the example of Melchizedek, priest of the high God

bringing a blessing to Abraham from outside the Jewish people (Gen. 14:18–20). And there is the incident of Jethro, father-in-law of Moses and priest of Midian, telling Moses, "Take my advice, and God will be with you ... if you do this — and may God so command you ... ," and quite fearlessly bringing to the great Jewish lawgiver a word of truth from outside the sacred arena of Judaism (Exod. 18:19, 23). The story of the prophets is the story of persons chosen by God to prophesy against the kings and priests and Temple, the restless descendants of the desert people speaking out against those who had settled down in the midst of their godless edifices and were satisfied with their lives and no longer searching for truth and for God.

John the Baptist, another son of the desert, lashed out at the religious leaders of his time and the party of the high priests: "Brood of vipers, who warned you to flee from the retribution that is coming? ... Even now the axe is laid to the roots of the trees, so that any tree which fails to produce good fruit will be cut down and thrown on the fire" (Mt. 3:8, 10).

Jesus was not a Temple person, not even allowed into the Holy of Holies. His conflict with the people of the Temple and his action of cleansing the Temple — really the prerogative of the priests, and not of an outsider like Jesus — contributed greatly to his death sentence. And once, in an argument with a feisty Samaritan woman over which was the proper place for worship, the Temple in Jerusalem or the sacred mountain of Samaria, Jesus proclaimed that the hour had come to worship God neither in the Temple of Jerusalem nor in any temple or on any holy mountain, but that the Spirit would lead us to the true worship of God — that God would be worshiped everywhere in spirit and in truth.

The bottom line seems to be that the word of prophecy and the word of truth are spoken outside the temple, not inside the temple. And it has always been so. It was so at the time of the first crisis in the early church, with its leaders clustered around the Temple in Jerusalem, reluctant to look outside that Temple for the revelation of the Spirit of Christ. It is true in our time with churchpeople fearfully clinging to the Christian temple as the only sanctuary of truth despite the meaning of Vatican Council II in pointing outside itself to the center of gravity located in the arena of the world, despite the clear voice of prophecy ringing out in our world today—outside the temple.

We continue to look for the meaning of the gospel and of the church, and its sacramental ministry, inside the church, inside the sacramental signs. So much reflection, so many treatments of the sacraments today still look for the deepest and final meaning of the sacraments within the community of believers—as if, were we to analyze thoroughly enough the love that these believers should have for one another psychologically, spiritually, liturgically, and in the light of faith, we would come to the complete significance of the sacraments. Meanwhile the sacraments slip more and more into insignificance in the life of the people. Is it possible that the true and ultimate meaning of the church, and the final meaning of the sacraments, can be found only *outside* the church, in the arena of the world, in the midst of creation?

Is such a thought outlandish? Did not St. Thomas Aquinas say that the Father has spoken only one time, and speaks that Word still. It is just that we hear that Word twice. The first time we hear it, it is the Son, the Word spoken from all eternity. The second time we hear it, it is creation, our world of created things.[1]

"You are my beloved Son. This day have I begotten you."

"Let there be light." Let there be a world.

Are these two words, or just one Word heard two times? If our world issues from that same one Word spoken by God which begets the Son of God, would it seem strange to find in that world the final meaning of our church and our sacraments? The world is the body of God.

What would all this mean for our understanding of the sacraments? The theology of the sacraments and the ministry of the sacraments would not revolve around deciding who has the power to administer them in the temple or the church or the sanctuary or at the altar, nor would it be about how much grace is accumulated by those allowed to receive them or about how many times they should receive them, nor even about the most effective liturgical manner in which to carry them out. Their ultimate meaning would lie not within the sign, not within the individual receiving them, not within the church—but outside, in the midst of human life. The most important ministry of the sacraments would be carried on out there, not around a temple or an altar.

We have been accustomed to going in the opposite direction in our handling and reception of the sacraments — away from the world. We have often thought of baptism and penance and even the Eucharist as saving us from an impure world, and certainly we have considered holy orders as a means of separating one from the world if not of escaping from it altogether. Our very language betrays us.

It is as if a sacrament were a kind of church building or temple into which we flee to get away from a sinful world. All holiness is found within that sanctuary, and outside, all is darkness and evil. A sacrament protects us and fortifies us with goodness. The more often we receive it, the better it is for us, the holier we are, the safer we are. And when we are finished receiving it, fortified and sanctified, we go back to that evil world, which just happens to be our human life. *Ite missa est.* Go, the Mass is ended.

No amount of liturgical emendation is going to correct a basic unsoundness in the direction of our sacramental ministry — erroneous in its almost magical appreciation of the sacraments, false in our own experience of receiving those sacraments, untrue in its view of God's world. Karl Rahner says that in a sacrament, "rather than entering a temple which walls off the holy from the godless world outside, man sets up in the open expanse of God's world a sign proclaiming that not in Jerusalem alone — but everywhere in spirit and truth, God is adored and experienced."[2]

It is to that open expanse of God's world that we must now turn our attention. If, as has been said, humankind has come of age, then it is time for the sacraments to come of age. We no longer talk as a child, eat as a child, dress as a child, read the books of a child, sing the songs of a child — but we often continue in the life of faith as a child for all our days. It is not a desirable situation.

"When I was a child, I used to talk like a child, and think like a child, and argue like a child, but now I am a man, all childish ways are put behind me" (1 Cor. 13:11). A child has to be a child, the center of its own world, reaching out gradually first to parents and relatives, and then to friends, schoolmates, and teachers, and finally to the world beyond. And there might well be a childlike manner of receiving the sacraments—in a kind of self-centered way, feeling a fearful awe at being forgiven one's childish sins and selfishness, experiencing physical elation at being one-on-one with Jesus in Communion. But never to leave that childlike state in our life of faith, to reach adulthood with identically the same religious mentality we had when we were eleven years old, is to be severely stunted in spiritual growth.

"Brothers, you are not to be childish in your outlook. You can be babies as far as wickedness is concerned, but mentally you must be adult" (1 Cor. 14:20). Sometimes we dispense or receive the sacraments with the self-centeredness of children. And when we do not experience that gratification, that elation, that immediate response, we feel a terrible emptiness, a growing doubt about the efficacy of the sacraments, and we imagine that we are losing our faith. We are no longer convinced of the *physical* presence of Christ in Communion, as we were as children, and we are afraid we no longer believe in the Eucharist. We may well be losing the faith of our childhood, with nothing to replace it. We become immature, crippled believers and Christians.

"We are all to come to unity in our faith and in our knowledge of the Son of God, until we become the perfect Man, fully mature with the fullness of Christ himself. Then we shall not be children any longer, or tossed one way and another and carried along by every wind of doctrine" (Eph. 4:13–14). It is difficult to arrive at the maturity of realizing that the God we pray to will be a silent God, as silent as a winter night or a breathless desert noontime. We get no answer to our prayer. We hear no voice of God. It requires maturity to realize that God does indeed respond to us, does answer us, does speak to us, as God has always done, in that primary locale of revelation—in creation, in the universe, in the world of created human beings that surround us. To grow from childhood, as a Christian, we have to look at the world in order to understand God and the sacraments of God, and in order to enter into dialogue with God there.

The world is not static. It is alive with history, with a story—monstrous at times—of greed and cruelty and selfishness and superficiality and stupidity and hatred, on one side; and a beautiful story of silent dedication, innocent suffering, faithfulness unto death, unbelievable devotion and sacrifice, selfless love, courage, joy, and sorrow, on the other. It is not only a story. It is a liturgy, a terrifying, sublime death and immolation liturgy celebrated by God. It reaches its ultimate meaning and culmination in the liturgy of the Son of God on the cross.[3] Looking at Jesus of Nazareth on the cross you see the liturgy of the world, all the monstrosity that put him there, all the beauty and unbelievable love that kept him there. This is not poetry. This is history, and the liturgy of our world, and the meaning of all liturgy and of every sacrament.

The sacraments must be as real as that world. We experience that world every day. We know that cruelty and greed and selfishness and hatred. It is as real to us as the daily newspaper and the evening news on television and our family life. It stuns us and shakes our faith to see such evil in the world. Where is God, and is there a God in the midst of all this? Yet, at the same time we know just as truly, in our own lives and in the lives of those around us, of that selfless, quiet devotion and indescribable love. That darkness-and-light reality is the basis of our liturgy and our sacraments.

"Until the Lord comes, therefore, every time you eat this bread and drink this cup, you are proclaiming his death" (1 Cor. 11:26). We proclaim the death of the Lord to those outside the church because there is death already present in the world, and the death of the Lord is the only thing that gives meaning to it. Even at that very moment when we might be tempted to think that we have escaped from the world, at that sacred moment of communion with Christ—especially at that moment—when we eat that bread and drink that cup, we are reaching out to that world in proclamation, announcing the only hope that world will ever have.

"Until he comes"—the coming of the Lord is whatever brings the world closer to its goal, closer to what God always meant it to be. Whatever brings the world closer to that goal is sacramental ministry, not just what happens in the sacred temple area. We lock ourselves into a mentality that defines sacramental ministry solely by its proximity to altar and sanctuary and temple. So much energy is expended in tension and controversy determining just who has the power and authority to *dispense* the sacraments, as if they were medicine to be doled out by a licensed physician. Who has the power to say the words of consecration, the words of absolution—priests or lay people, male or female? Who has the authority to baptize? Who can preside? Who can anoint? Who can preach and read the Word of God in liturgy? Who can bless? Who can serve Mass—boys or girls? All of this refers to activities swirling around an altar or sanctuary or baptismal font. All these questions refer to reform or renewal of the church—many changes or prescriptions to be carried out on the same single level; countless laws and details that end up tiring us, discouraging us. None of these details has anything to do with *refounding* the church, lifting the whole matter to an entirely different level, away from the sanctuary and altar, out into the midst of human life.

It has been pointed out that the word "sacrament" is not mentioned in the New Testament. It is probably just as well that it is not. Instead, the Gospels are filled with the meaning of sacrament and sacramentality, and the arena for these New Testament sacraments is far from Temple and synagogue. The baptism that is described takes place along the winding river Jordan, which snakes its way through the dry Palestinian countryside, not far from the desert: "What did you go out into the desert to see?" Jesus performed the sacramental ministry of matrimony—supplying necessities for celebration—in the midst of human homes, at a wedding feast.

It was in the wilderness again that Jesus took part in another sacred action: supplying bread for the hungry and explaining the sacramental meaning of the bread—a sign pointing to "the living bread come down from heaven." And at the well of Samaria, he used the water as a sign of the Spirit, the living water that will quench every thirst: "Anyone who drinks the water that I shall give will never be thirsty again: the water that I shall give will turn into a spring inside him, welling up to eternal life" (Jn. 4:13–14).

Perhaps the place in the Gospels that most clearly portrays Christ as teaching about the sacraments, and enjoining their use upon us, is the time of the resurrection. Each apparition of Christ after Easter is linked dramatically to the sacraments as we know them or, at least, as we should know them. It is as if Christ were explaining, "Now that the resurrection is a reality and you apostles and disciples have been witnesses to it, this is the way you have to pass on, and have others share in, the new creation that has dawned on the world":

Go to my brothers—[you will find me there] [Jn. 20:17; Mt. 28:7; Mk. 16:7].

Make disciples of all nations; baptize them in the name of the Father and of the Son and of the Holy Spirit [Mt. 28:19].

Go out to the whole world; proclaim the Good News to all creation [Mk. 16:16].

Receive the Holy Spirit. Whose sins you shall forgive, they are forgiven [Jn. 20:22–23].

Did not our hearts burn within us as he talked to us on the road and explained the scriptures to us? [Lk. 24:32].

You see how it is written that the Christ would suffer and on the third day rise from the dead, and that, in his name, repentance for the forgiveness of sins would be preached to all the nations. . . . You are witnesses to this [Lk. 24:46–48].

They had recognized him at the breaking of bread [Lk. 24:35].

Feed my lambs. . . . Feed my sheep [Jn. 21:15, 17].

These appearances of the risen One, and the commands to sacramental action, were not made in synagogue or Temple, but in the most profoundly human—almost idyllically human—situations:

—A cheerful greeting to women in a garden on the first Sunday morning.

—An encounter with a beloved friend in the same garden.

—A walk down a country lane with friends on a Sunday afternoon.

—Dinner at a village inn as evening descended.

—A meal with friends in an upper room already filled with meaning by the last meal held there.

—Intense interest in friends' human livelihood and occupation of fishing and some advice on how to do it more effectively.

—Cooking breakfast for friends, and breakfasting with them by the lakeside, after a hard night's work.

—Calling forth from a friend a deeply moving triple profession of human love: "Lord, you know that I love you."

What are these Gospel stories trying to tell us? And why is it that we never seem to hear it? Are they saying that this is a redeemed world? That grace is really guiding the history of the world? That the world is permanently graced at its roots, whether we accept that reality or not? That grace is not a phenomenon occurring parallel to the rest of human life, but is part of human life, that it is the holiness of all that is profane?[4]

In contrast to this New Testament message, we often pass on as sacramental catechesis something very different, saying in effect that the world is brutally and hopelessly profane and evil, and that in receiving the sacraments we are momentarily transcending that evil and profane world. If we do this, we are making a pretense of stepping out of this evil world into a sacred area, a kind of make-believe that will not last long in an adult's life and could lead to the most desolate loss of faith in the efficacy of sacraments and sacred symbols. Karl Rahner says of the sacramental sign: "It is a perpetual tragic misunderstanding when this little sign, which is to remind us of the limitlessness of God's grace, is made into an enclosure in which alone God and his grace are to be found."[5]

We have to try to understand how unreal the church and Christianity and Christ can seem to ordinary members of a Catholic parish today in an increasingly secularized world. Many people remain in a parish today simply out of a blind loyalty, from a kind of primal need for bonding and belonging, with little understanding of, and little interest or even faith in, the message of Christianity or of the church and its ministry. Church leaders

seem unaware, or unwilling to become aware, of the dismal situation of the faith life of its members, and indeed of many of
its priests. These church leaders often act as if it were forty
years earlier, or a hundred or more years earlier, instead of
being on the brink of the twenty-first century.

It is sadly ironic that church leaders today still refuse to give
their blessing to inter-communion with Protestants because
"*they* do not believe what *we* believe about the Eucharist," when
there is the great probability that there is as much divergence
among Catholics concerning Eucharist as there is between Catholics and Protestants. And when you come to baptism, the faith
situation becomes more unreal. As regards confession and confirmation, the reality disappears altogether. One has to be a
pastor, not a sociologist, to realize this today.

To refound the church for a new age, a revision of the ritual
will hardly be enough. "You must render an account of your
belief," St. Paul said. We must render an account that is credible
not only to ourselves, but to others and to our age. For an
increasingly sophisticated and educated Christian community, a
childish, patronizing, unreal presentation of the sacraments,
having nothing to do with the world in which Christians live, will
not suffice. Efforts have been made since Vatican Council II to
make the sacraments more real and more understandable to a
new age. We must have the courage to continue those efforts,
not to reform or revitalize the understanding of the sacraments
but to lift that understanding to an entirely different level.

BAPTISM

We of this age are the first people, not just to know but to
experience that we are adrift in space. One of the things that
helped all of us to share in this experience and realization was
that beautiful picture taken from space of this blue and brown
and white planet, lonely against the vast black background of
endless space. It was the first picture we ever saw of a redeemed
planet. We have seen some close-up pictures of other planets.
We don't know much about them otherwise, but they *looked*, at
least, like frighteningly unredeemed planets. We have shown an
incredible interest in the possibility of life on other planets,

inside and outside our solar system. We know nothing about life on any other planet, but we know a great deal about life on that lovely blue and white and brown planet called earth. We know that life on that planet is redeemed life, that it is a redeemed planet; we know that the only kind of sin on that planet is forgiven sin, that the resurrection has already begun on that planet, that the planet earth is already part of the new creation, that the Christ has meaning for that entire planet. This is our faith. This is what we believe.

When we talk about baptism, it must have meaning for, and relationship to, that entire planet or it has no meaning at all. If it means initiation into membership in the church, then we have to say the same thing about the church. Somehow that church has to be a visible sign that this is indeed a redeemed planet, a sign meant for all its inhabitants that this globe is bathed in salvation, that it is saved—"the sign of salvation held up for all the nations."

Baptism is the initiation rite of membership in the community of Christ on the earth. That community of Christ is a sign of the community of humankind, the human community. Both communities are symbolized here. The ritual action is a bathing or a drowning, a dying and coming to life again. If it is an infant baptism, we are celebrating the innocence of that child, a member of a fallen human race who has taken no part in the evil of that race; the child is a sign of that race's salvation and beauty, just as the church—of which that child is today made a member—is a sign of humankind's beauty and salvation. If it is an adult baptism, then the conversion of that adult (a conversion necessary for the validity of that baptism) has the same significance as that of the child: salvation, redemption of the entire human race.

Water stands for much more than just quenching our thirst and cleansing us. Constantly recurring stories of terrible flooding in different parts of the world remind us that water can be devastating, destructive, and killing. Water is part of creation groaning and travailing even until now, waiting for the revelation of the sons and daughters of God, yearning to be released from that slavery to decadence, just like us, as St. Paul explains, hoping to be free to enjoy the same salvation and glory of the children of God. It is an apt symbol of dying and rising. We Christians led the pack in desacralizing nature, and then in despoiling it. In baptism we can begin to restore it to its sacred vocation.

Liturgy of the World in Baptism

Human community has been violently shattered by the escalation of sin in the world from the beginning of history, and as recently as the evening news. Rampant economic, political, social, and religious individualism has reduced community to tatters. That is the death. And the life? Forgiveness of sins, those same sins, is one of the major fruits of the New Testament.

What does salvation mean in such a situation? Primarily, it means the restoration of that broken community, which takes us beyond the church out into the world. In other words, when we talk about salvation in reference to baptism, we are not focusing on the salvation of the one being baptized, but on the salvation of the human community. The salvation of the one being baptized, as real as it might be, is primarily a sign of that far greater redemption. A person is not baptized for himself or herself, but for others. We find the deepest meaning of baptism outside the sign, outside the church. It is a reminder of the limitlessness of God's grace, not a cage that holds it captive.

We tend to look at the good and beautiful that happen outside the church and sacraments as exceptional, freakish, unexplainable, not worthy of our praise and admiration. Yet that is the meaning of the church—the sign of salvation held up for the nations and the world—proclaiming that indeed God and divine grace are active in the world. Every time a person acts in a truly human way, grace is there, is active. Every time a person laughs in joy, cries in sorrow, accepts responsibility, loves what is beautiful, stands up for truth, breaks away from selfishness, hopes, refuses to be embittered and to despair as all around are doing—there is grace, there is salvation. These are remarkable accomplishments. Young people and many others outside the church sense that they are accomplishments, yet they are made to feel that these "natural" accomplishments lie outside the pale of Christianity and the church instead of being reminded that the function of the church is to point to these things and their grace-filled value. Grace is everywhere. The hour is already here when, not in the Temple of Jerusalem, nor in any temple, but everywhere in spirit and in truth, God is being experienced and worshiped. God *wants* such worshipers, Jesus said. If we were to discover a race of intelligent beings on another planet who stood up for truth and accepted responsibility for their actions and who had hope, we would say that they were obviously a redeemed race. Is our own race any less worthy of celebration?

The Baptismal Sign

The baptismal rite of initiation into the community of Christ, with its cleansing and dying and rising, must incorporate the liturgy of the world in its own liturgy.

"What do you ask of the church of God as this child is about to be baptized?"

"*Faith.*"

Faith in what? Belief in what? Belief that it is necessary in our society to have a child baptized in order to appear at all respectable and decent and Christian? Belief that the waters of baptism will save this child from the fires of hell, or from an eternity of limbo, or from the grip of the devil by whom it is now enslaved? Does any mother in the world believe that? Then why do we celebrate such a belief in our liturgy? Our liturgy must make sense and speak sense to the American people and to all people. Is not the faith of baptism the faith in that grace of God everywhere present and active in our world, a grace that can *never* be lost for our world?[6] Are we not celebrating the innocence of that child, the innocence of that converted and baptized adult, as a sign of the grace and innocence and salvation being regained by a fallen world? If we do not believe in that grace of God acting in the world even outside the church, then we should abstain from baptism, because no sacrament is valid without faith.

The Ministry of Baptism

Since the ultimate and deepest meaning of baptism lies outside the sign itself, so should the most meaningful ministry of baptism lie outside. Everything that builds up the community of

Christ is baptismal, everything that makes that community a sign of unity, a bond of love; everything that makes the members of that community vitally interrelated to one another so that the fate of one lies in the hands of the others, so that whatever truly affects one for good or evil affects all just as deeply; everything that enables the members of that community to discern the body of Christ in the community, so that, when they gather for Eucharist, it is indeed the Lord's Supper they are making—all this is baptismal ministry.

But this community of Christ is just a sign of an even deeper community, the community of humankind, for the sake of which the community of Christ is in the world. Every activity that builds up, sustains, heals that human community is baptismal ministry. It is time for us to leave our sacramental ghetto and to go out into our neighborhoods, our society, the world and help to restore our shattered community. Americans are among the loneliest people in the world, in desperate need of community.

We are the community of Christ, a people whose vocation is to be a credible witness and sign of what a human community is supposed to be. The people among whom we live exist in terrible fear of crime and violence and exploitation and economic uncertainty. They lock themselves in their homes as protection for themselves and their possessions. They buy terrible weapons of destruction to defend themselves. They give up— block by block, street by street, park by park—their cities as viable places of human habitation. They refuse to become involved in the desperate needs of their neighbors or to depend in any way on their neighbors for their own needs. Such an involvement or dependence would go against the grain of American individualism, the destructive creed of the land. If they are financially able, they move away to a place where they will never again have to be connected to their neighbors' houses by sidewalks. America's most urgent need is community.

Nevertheless, the liturgy of the world continues. Despite all this darkness there is light in the midst of it: remarkable efforts of pulling away from selfishness and fear and despair; grace-filled and graceful actions of self-sacrifice and devotion and love are seen in work with the elderly, the homeless, the meal-less, with runaway youth and the handicapped and alcoholics. Holy work. It is our vocation to join with this refusal to despair and to point out to all those involved, "there has stood one in your midst whom you have not recognized," and to see in all of it the meaning of our baptism. Without it, our baptismal sign is empty—a vacuum. The baptismal sign must reflect the liturgy of the world where sin and faithfulness come face to face. The baptismal sign must proclaim to us that, without Christ, human-kind's hope is vain, and that, without humankind, Christ is an abstract ideology.

St. Paul describes the liturgy of the world and the meaning of our baptismal ministry: "And for anyone who is in Christ, there is a new creation; the old creation has gone, and now the new one is here. It is all God's work. . . . In other words, God in Christ was reconciling the world to himself, not holding men's faults against them, and he has entrusted to us the news that they are reconciled. So we are ambassadors for Christ" (2 Cor. 5:17–20).

Paul depicts in moving language the vocation of these heralds of Good News, these ambassadors of Christ, a vocation that proclaims the victory of grace, a grace that can never again be lost for our world, despite all the appearances of defeat: "They call us deceivers, yet we tell the truth; unknown but we are fully acknowledged; dying men and see we live; punished but not condemned to death; sad men who rejoice continually; beggars who bring riches to many; disinherited, and the world is ours" (2 Cor. 5:8–10).

EUCHARIST

If any one sacrament stands for the whole of Christianity and the church, it is the Eucharist. It is the one sacrament that symbolizes fully what the Christian message is, what it means for the world. Indeed it points to the world and all creation. It speaks for all the Bible from the food of the tree of life in the primeval garden to the messianic banquet at the end time; from the blood of goats and heifers of the Old Covenant to the blood of the New Covenant. It is the presence of God in the world. It is the cross and the resurrection of Christ. It is the forgiveness of sins and reconciliation. It is salvation and the new creation.

It is inexhaustible. It is Shalom. It is the breakthrough in the spiritualization of the material world. It is the ultimate destination toward which all the religions of the world, with all their sacred symbols from the beginning of time, have been tending and striving. It is what the Jewish high priest and the American Indian shaman, and the Hindu priest, and the Teutons and the Celts, and the African witch doctors have been trying to say. It is what Jesus *did* say: "All this is my body." This is a sacrament that should never be trivialized by clerical usurpation, mindless repetition, deadening automatic ritual, individualized piety, or narrow sacralization.

Liturgy of the World in the Eucharist

St. John, in the Fourth Gospel, unforgettably depicts the liturgy of the world of this sacrament: "In the beginning was the Word: The Word was with God and the Word was God. ... Through him all things came to be, not one thing had its being but through him. ... He was in the world that had its being through him, and the world did not know him. ... The Word was made flesh and dwelt among us. ... This flesh is food indeed ... and the bread that I shall give is my flesh for the life of the world" (Jn. 1 and 6, passim).

The world and its creator are in dialogue. God spoke one Word and it is God's Son and our world. The whole history of the world, of everything that happens in salvation history, from the beginning to the end, is the reality beneath the sacrament (*res sacramenti*) of the Eucharist. The world is offering itself up, is already being offered up, in triumph and tears and blood to God.[7] Vatican Council II moved our attention away from the confection of the sacrament, or the ritual surrounding it, to the celebration of the sacrament, to the quality of participation required. It lays heavy stress on the Eucharist as a self-conscious self-articulation of the whole quality of life in community, as an honest assessment and confession of who we are, positively and negatively, of the love that builds up and the sin that tears apart the "sign of unity and bond of love" that we are supposed to be.[8]

The Sign of the Eucharist

Vatican Council II not only turns our attention away from emphasizing the powers of confection, but also leads us away from the "magic moment of consecration" to the entire liturgical action of the assembly as the sign of the Eucharist, as the sign of the presence of Christ throughout the entire time of the Lord's Supper. *Because* two or more of us gather in Christ's name, *because* we open ourselves to God's Word, *because* we break bread together, we believe that the risen Christ is in our midst; and he is in our midst not only at the consecration but also throughout the entire liturgy, just as he was with the two disciples both at the breaking of the bread in Emmaus, and also as they walked toward the village on resurrection afternoon.[9]

In the midst of the canon of the Mass we announce or sing, "Let us proclaim the mystery of faith." We sometimes take this proclamation very lightly, but the *mystery of faith* is essential to authentic Eucharist. It is this call to belief that gives meaning to the Eucharist. The death and resurrection of Christ; the destruction of despair of our own death and the building up of our hope for life; the proclamation of the death of the Lord to this century of death and spilling of blood which is like no century before it; this dearly bought freedom and the saving of our world are the content of this mystery of faith, of this liturgy of the world. We can offer up the world with the bread and the wine only because the world is already being offered up.

This mystery of faith exists not just in the sacred host, but in the *gathering* of those called to be the "sign of salvation for the nations." It exists in the *Word* that is proclaimed, the message hidden from the foundation of the world that will break down the barrier between the nations, a barrier that threatens to destroy us all. The Eucharistic sign must point to that mystery in our lives or it is an empty sign—it is no Eucharist at all. We must have that sacramental vision in our lives or we cannot celebrate it in Eucharist. We can receive the true body of Christ only if we are in communion with the body of God—the world and its fate.[10] That mystery must become so real that we can celebrate it. If we do not celebrate it, if we do not express it, it becomes irrelevant. It ceases to function. And so does Eucharist.

In the Gospel of John, Thomas the apostle is depicted as "doubting Thomas" during resurrection week. He does not believe that Jesus is risen just because the other apostles say they have seen him. He wants to see for himself, to put his finger and his hand into the wounds just to make sure. We tend to ridicule him for his lack of faith, and to distance ourselves from any identification with him in our faith life. We prefer to be identified with "those who have not seen and have believed." Yet we recognize that need of his.

Thomas was asking for a more sacramental awareness of the risen Christ. He wanted to see and touch for himself. And as a result of that seeing and that invitation to touch, he rose to the greatest height of faith shown in the Gospel stories, greater than any other apostle. No other apostle called Jesus "my Lord and my God."

Ash Wednesday is one of the most popular liturgical feast days on college campuses across America, despite our rather fastidious and enlightened efforts to downplay it as superstitious and superficial. Young people feel comfortable at a ceremony designed specifically for sinners and in which they can participate fully without feeling hypocritical. The best part about it, they say, is that "the priest reaches out and touches us." The dirty ashes are as earthy as an open wound in the hands or in the side.

Blessed are we who have not seen and have believed; but we need to see and touch also—and to be seen and touched. That is the sign of the Eucharist, the sign of the *gathering* of sinners who believe, the sign of the *Word* of hope about a sinful world redeemed, the sign of the bread and body broken for us. *Mysterium fidei!*

The Ministry of the Eucharist

The authentic ministers of the Eucharist are not cluttered around an altar. They are in the world, in the midst of human life, and they need no permission or authorization from bishop or priest to carry out their ministry. They received their authorization in baptism. This is not said to take sides in the question as to who has the authority to confect the sacramental sign in the sanctuary, priest or lay person. It is to point out, rather, that the main and primary Eucharistic ministry is not performed in the sanctuary at all, but outside the sanctuary walls—in the world. If that ministry is not performed outside, the sacramental sign is empty and meaningless.

What is that Eucharistic ministry outside the sanctuary? Everyone admits that chapter 6 of the Gospel of John is entirely Eucharistic. And what is it about, that chapter 6? It is about feeding a multitude of hungry people in the wilderness:

> It was shortly before the Jewish feast of Passover. Looking up, Jesus saw the crowds approaching and said to Philip, "Where can we buy some bread for these people to eat? . . . Make the people sit down." There was plenty of grass there, and as many as five thousand people sat down. Then Jesus took the loaves, gave thanks, and gave them out to all who were sitting ready; he then did the same with the fish, giving out as much as was wanted. When they had eaten enough he said to the disciples, "Pick up the pieces left over, so that nothing gets wasted." So they picked them up, and filled twelve hampers with scraps left over from the meal of five barley loaves [Jn. 6:3–5, 10, 13].

It is hardly a laborious or tortuous step from this reading to say that feeding hungry people is Eucharistic ministry, especially since Jesus makes this very action the criterion for entering the kingdom in the Last Judgment story: "I was hungry and you gave me to eat. . . . As long as you did it for one of the least of my brethren, you did it for me."

The Eucharistic bread is an empty symbol if the hungry are not fed, and it will never be a completely authentic symbol of the body of Christ as long as there are hungry people anywhere in the world. The action of feeding the hungry is Eucharistic ministry, whether it is done on a private level or a government level. Soup kitchens, Meals on Wheels for the elderly, and aid for the starving children of Africa is Eucharistic ministry. It can be visible and heroic, like Catholic Relief Services and rock concert benefits, or anonymous and equally heroic like the love and compassion of the Good Samaritan. The very carrying out of such a ministry in such circumstances by a Christian defines authentically the proper place of the church in the world of today and tomorrow. The vision of faith of a Christian, the *mysterium fidei*, the awareness of the liturgy of the world going on, inspires an integrity and compassionate love so essential to that work where it is lacking, and reinforces it when it is present in good and decent human beings, whatever their faith, or lack of it might be. In a Christianity come of age, the church assumes its proper place not in a sanctuary, but in the midst of human life.

The Gospel story of John, interestingly and aptly enough, also shows what to do with surplus food: treat it with the same reverence shown the twelve baskets of bread left over after the feeding of the multitudes in the desert, so that, as Jesus says, "nothing gets wasted." There is even more to this Eucharistic story than that:

> Jesus answered the crowd: "I tell you most solemnly, you are not looking for me because you have seen the signs but because you had all the bread you wanted to eat. Do not work for food that cannot last, but work for food that endures to eternal life, the kind of food the Son of Man is offering you, ... for the bread of God is that which comes down from heaven and gives life to the world. ... I am the bread of life. He who comes to me will never be hungry; he who believes in me will never thirst. ... I am the living bread which has come down from heaven. Anyone who eats this bread will live forever; and the bread that I shall give is my flesh, for the life of the world" [Jn. 6:26–27, 35, 51].

Jesus explains the sacramental meaning of the bread he has fed the multitudes. It points to that which nourishes the deepest possible kind of life. It points to the life of the world itself. Jesus is extending the meaning of Eucharist to its furthest bounds. It is not our feeble effort that identifies the limits of the Eucharist as the world itself. It is the vision of Jesus that does this. He mentions his flesh, which John has already identified with the Word at the beginning of time, the same flesh that will be torn apart on the cross—for the world. There is something cosmic involved here. The Eucharist, the bread, the flesh of Christ, represents and encompasses all of creation. That might sound far-fetched, overly ambitious, overblown, and simplistically poetic. How can the entire universe of created things be contained in a single symbol? How indeed?

The idea is no more simplistic, or ambitious, or all-encompassing than the conclusion to which the physical scientists are becoming more assuredly drawn in their own exciting discipline—that all of creation as we know it originated in a particle smaller than an atom, a particle containing an almost infinite source of energy, the "big bang of creation." All the fiber of our being was contained in that particle; every synapse of our brain, all our world, all human history, every human accomplishment, every artistic achievement, every note of music, every sin that was ever committed were in the original particle at the dawn of creation. "All this is my body."

Scientists are becoming more and more reverent, more filled with awe and wonder, less hostile to religion, the closer they come to understanding that original explosion of creation. And well they should be less hostile. The notion of one God preserved by Jewish and Christian and Islamic tradition contributed greatly to the atmosphere of searching for one source and one explanation for the entire universe. The concept of the universe proposed by all these great religions (different things represented by a single idea, or one idea applicable to different things—*unum versus alia*) is the breeding ground for the theory of a single, indescribably powerful origin of all creation.

We Christians would rather refer to that origin as the "original Word" spoken just once, but heard two times by us—the first time as the only begotten Son, and the second time as the "big bang" of creation. It is fascinating to think that these scientists probing toward an ultimate unity in the physical world lead us to the unity beyond, which is in reality the *community* that lies at the heart of everything that exists—Father, Son, and Holy Spirit—Father and Son in that eternal dialogue of the spoken Word, and the Spirit hovering over the darkness, the emptiness, the vacuum, the nothingness (the *Tohu Bohu*, the trackless wastes) at the beginning of creation. Scientists owe a great deal to religion. Copernicus was a churchman. Galileo (The Galilean) was a devout Christian. The investigation of the meaning of the universe is Eucharistic ministry. Christians should continue at the heart of it.

Sincere and compassionate efforts at preserving our planet from nuclear or poisonous destruction are Eucharistic ministry at its most basic and obvious level. The words of Christ concerning the Eucharist take on a poignant and urgent meaning for the people of our age, a meaning that perhaps would have been incomprehensible to men and women of another age: "The bread of God is that which comes down from heaven and gives life to the world . . . and the bread that I shall give is my flesh, for the life of the world" (Jn. 6:27, 51).

If this particular ministry is not carried out successfully, we shall obviously come to the end of Eucharist. The Eucharistic ministry should be a ministry of stewardship, not ownership, of the things of the earth. Christians should recognize the reverence for life evidenced in the culture of the American Indians and the Asian Indians and the animist Africans, and be willing to learn from them. This ministry ought to strive to lead Americans away from the crass notion that if they have enough money they can actually buy a lake or a mountain or a stretch of the earth's seashores for their own exclusive use. If Christians do not understand stewardship—that we truly own nothing, but are privileged to use the world with reverence and pass it on with care to future generations—then who will understand it? We Christians have led humankind in despoiling the earth. We have stood at the heart of this original sin of humanity. In a Christianity come of age, we must stand in the forefront of every effort to save it.

"Preach the gospel to all creation." Those beautiful mysterious words of Christ, as recorded in Mark, speak of the ultimate in Eucharistic ministry. Scientists have been struck by the similarity in design between the medieval cathedral and the present-day particle accelerator. Both are monumental in structure, pushing to the limits and beyond the technology and science of their time. Both house tremendous mysteries: one, the mystery of the Eucharist; the other, the mystery of matter itself. And both are pointing and stretching upward and outward to the stars.

6

The Thirteenth Apostle

And there was a man who came to him and asked, "Master, what good deed must I do to possess eternal life?" Jesus said to him, "Why do you ask me about what is good? There is one alone who is good. But if you wish to enter into life, keep the commandments." He said, "Which?" "These," Jesus replied: "You must not kill. You must not commit adultery. You must not bring false witness. Honor your father and mother, and you must love your neighbor as yourself." The young man said to him, "I have kept all these. What more do I need to do?" Jesus said, "If you wish to be perfect, go and sell what you own and give the money to the poor, and you will have treasure in heaven; then come, follow me." But when the young man heard these words he went away sad, for he was a man of great wealth [Mt. 19:16–22].

When Karl Rahner described the post-Vatican Council II age as the third stage of the church, the epoch of the world church, he mentioned that until the time of Vatican II, the church had not made a dent in the great non-Christian religions of the world. Until that time there was no dialogue possible with these religions. Missionaries, facing Islam, Buddhism, and Hinduism, had discovered the same thing. Because of the attitude and policy of the church, missionaries working in the midst of these great religions had, as it were, their hands tied behind their backs. It was impossible to dialogue with, and thus evangelize, the people of these religions. They were asked to act as if the religion of these people was merely a small part of their lives, like the corner of a page folded down to mark the progress of one's reading. The turned-down corner did not really matter. You could still read the page with the corner folded down. That corner of a page was considered equivalent to the non-Christian religion that any particular people followed. The remaining part of the page was the rest of their lives. All you had to do, according to the church, was to remove that corner of non-Christian religion and replace it with the Christian religion, and you had a Christianized people. This was a great fallacy for one commanding reason: indigenous religion—whether it was Hinduism or Islam or even animism—permeated the entire life of the people who professed it. It filled their life from the time they got up in the morning until they went to bed at night. The only way to remove that religion from a people was to destroy that people, as individuals and as a culture. You would have had to destroy that Islamic nation or that animist tribe culturally and entirely. That religion was part and parcel of their lives, of their culture. Religion is part of the culture of any people and— as far as non-Christian religions go—the most important part. Christians, who like to keep religion to a minimum in their lives, might find this hard to believe. No wonder dialogue with the people of these religions has been impossible until now, because evangelization of these peoples would require the destruction of Hinduism and Islam and Buddhism and animism.

The missionary mandate of Christ does not decree a destruction of the nations and cultures of the world, but merely the bringing of the gospel to these cultures, as they are. When Jesus spoke about the Jewish culture, symbolized by the Jews' religion and their law, he said, "I did not come to do away with it, but to fulfill it." Vatican Council II marked the first time the church spoke of the great non-Christian religions of the world in a positive way, as repositories of truth and goodness.

RELIGION, REVELATION, AND FAITH

Religion is part of a culture. Christianity as a religion— whether Irish Catholic religion, or Spanish Catholic religion, or Roman Catholic religion—could never dialogue with these non-

Christian cultures and religions. Only as a *faith* can Christianity dialogue with them and evangelize them.

Revelation is what God wants us to know and to do, and faith is the authentic response to that revelation from the midst of our human lives. Religion is what *we make* of that revelation of what God wants us to know and to do. People of every culture receive revelation of what God wants us to know and to do. People of every culture receive revelation from God, either in the fleshy tablets of their hearts or from the Word of God, and they can respond to it in faith. And when they do, people of other faiths can recognize it as an authentic response to revelation—whether it be the humble worship of the one God of Africa, or the beautiful reverence for life of the American Indian and the Hindus, or the admirable and total submission to God of the Muslims, or the joy and hope of Christian peoples. But they can also take that authentic revelation of God and make it into something frightening—their own exclusive religion. Muslims have done it. Jews have done it. Other non-Christians have done it. And Christians have done it, too.

Sometimes authentic revelation still shines forth in that religion. Sometimes it does not. When it does not, that religion itself needs evangelization, whether it be Hinduism or Irish Catholicism—an evangelization carried out, of course, with the greatest reverence and sensitivity to that religion.

Several times, in the Gospels, Jesus speaks of turning God's revelation into religion, in the bad sense:

> Pharisees and scribes from Jerusalem then came to Jesus and said, "Why do your disciples break away from the tradition of the elders? They do not wash their hands when they eat food." "And why do you," he answered, "break away from the commandment of God for the sake of your tradition? For God said: Do your duty to your father and mother.... But you say, 'If anyone says to his father or mother: anything that I have that I might have used to help you is dedicated to God,' he is rid of his duty to father and mother. In this way you have made God's word null and void by means of your tradition. Hypocrites! It was you Isaiah meant when he so rightly prophesied: '*This peo-*

*ple honors me only with lip-service while their hearts are far
from me. The worship they offer me is worthless: the doctrines
they teach are only human regulations.'* . . . These are the
things that make a man unclean. But to eat with unwashed
hands does not make a man unclean" [Mt. 15:1–9, 20].

The revelation of God as related in the first book of the Bible,
and in the first story in the Bible, is quite clear. God makes clear
what humankind should know and do: "Be fruitful and multiply,
fill the earth and conquer it. . . . You may eat of all the trees in
the garden. Nevertheless, of the tree of the knowledge of good
and evil, you are not to eat." God saw all divine creation, "and
indeed it was very good"—which has to be the greatest under-
statement in the Bible. If God saw that it was very good, *it had
to be perfect*. The world was the way God meant it to be. And
there was no religion in the world.

Then in Genesis 3:1 everything changes. We have the first
religious question in the Bible: "Did God really say you were
not to eat from any of the trees in the garden?" God said no
such thing. The revelation of God was very clear. But with that
question, the serpent's question, religion enters the Bible and
human history.

After that, the Bible is filled with religious questions and
religious actions: Cain's question after slaughtering Abel, "Am
I my brother's keeper?"; the building of the tower of Babel to
reach up to God and become a people with a name; Moses'
questioning his calling, and the people in the desert yearning
for Egypt and worshiping the golden calf; the people of Israel
demanding a king and desiring a temple. Every religious question that was asked or implied further changed the revelation
of God into what people made of that revelation.

In his lifetime, as depicted in the Gospels, Jesus was plagued
with religious questions, directed at him or his disciples. Examples of such questions, just from the Gospel of Matthew,
include:

—Why does your master eat with tax collectors and sinners?

—Why is it that we and the Pharisees fast, but your disciples do not?

—Is it against the law to cure a person on the Sabbath day?

—Where did this man get this wisdom and these miraculous powers? Is not his mother called Mary and his brothers James and Joseph and Simon and Jude? His sisters, too, are they not all here with us?

—Why do your disciples break away from the tradition of the elders? They do not wash their hands when they eat.

—Lord, how often must I forgive my brother if he wrongs me? As often as seven times?

—Is it lawful for a man to divorce his wife on any pretext whatever?

Jesus' answer to the last question (in Mt. 19:8–9) clearly points out the distinction between revelation (what God wants us to know and to do) and religion (what we make of what God wants us to know and to do). God says No! Moses, because of the hardness of the people's hearts, says Yes!

And then, finally, the rich young man comes to Jesus with his religious question: "What good deed must I do to possess eternal life?" He is asking: *"What one action can I carry out to ensure my salvation?"* Not, "What orientation must I give to my life?" or, "What response must I make to God's goodness?" But, "What good deed must I do?" Never mind what God has revealed to us and what is written on the fleshy tablets of our hearts—"What good deed can we do, what law can we follow that will guarantee our entrance into heaven?"

Abstain from a certain food? Go to the Temple on a certain day? Say a certain set of prayers? Carry out a certain ritual? Fulfill certain regulations? Wear certain clothes? Repeat certain words in a special language? Carry out a certain devotion? Spin a prayer wheel? A pilgrimage? A trip to Mecca? Perform a holy action on a specified number of days—say three or nine? Increase the number of prayers, or the time allotted to them? People of every persuasion can surely recognize, in the young man's question, religious questions of their own.

Behind such religious questions, very often, hides something that we would much prefer to mask, something we would prefer not to be brought up. This obviously was true in the case of the young man. How he wanted Jesus to take him off the hook, so to speak, to give him "one good deed" to carry out, so that he could forget that one terrible obstacle standing between him and holiness. But Jesus led him to it: "Go sell what you own and give the money to the poor. . . . Then come, follow me."

The one thing the young man did not want to hear.

Religion comes from inside us. Revelation comes from outside us. Religion stabilizes and reassures us. Revelation destabilizes and disturbs us. Revelation calls into question everything solid and taken for granted. Religion so often tries to use God as a means to a human end. It calls on God to bless every conceivable project. It makes God a projection of self rather than the God of biblical revelation. Religion is filled with answers to every question. The God of the Bible is a divine questioner, not an answerer.[1]

The rich young man received the very same call as Peter and James and John and Matthew: "Come, follow me." The demand of renunciation was not new or unique. All the apostles experienced it.

As [Jesus] was walking by the sea of Galilee he saw two brothers, Simon, who was called Peter, and his brother Andrew; they were making a cast in the lake with their net, for they were fishermen. And he said to them, "Follow me. . . ." And they left their nets at once and followed him. Going on from there he saw another pair of brothers, James son of Zebedee and his brother John; they were in their boat with their father Zebedee, mending their nets, and he called them. At once, leaving the boat and their father, they followed him [Mt. 4:18–22].

Matthew, or Levi as he is called by Luke, reacted to the call in the same way: "When [Jesus] went out after this, he noticed a tax collector, Levi by name, sitting by the custom house, and said to him, 'Follow me.' And leaving everything he got up and followed him" (Lk. 5:27–28).

Peter at one point makes specific reference to the renunciation involved in following Jesus: "Then Peter spoke. 'What about us?' he said to [Jesus]. 'We have left everything and followed you. What are we to have, then?' " (Mt. 19:27).

Jesus did not play games, or pretend, with people. He issued a real call to that young man. Mark, in relating that story, adds a beautiful detail: "Jesus looked steadily at him and loved him" (Mk. 10:20). The story has the same personal quality about it as the description of Jesus' first meeting with the two men, Andrew and John, in the Fourth Gospel, men who would become his apostles: "Jesus turned around, saw them following and said, 'What is it you want?' They answered, 'Rabbi'—which means teacher—'Where do you live?' 'Come and see,' he replied; so they went and saw where he lived, and stayed with him the rest of the day. It was about the tenth hour" (Jn. 1:38–39).

Jesus did not give a religious answer to the rich young man's religious question. His response turned the young man away from a deed or an action to a person: "Come, follow me." He did not ask the young man to carry out the renunciation demanded of him in isolation, relying on his own strength. The invitation Jesus extended was for the young man to work out his response in community. He was invited to walk in the company of Jesus, a companion especially loved by him, perhaps like John, the beloved disciple. And he turned down that call—because of his possessions. This is somehow shabbier than denying Jesus out of fear, as Peter did. One can only wonder just how many possessions the young man had that would have justified his refusal to be the thirteenth apostle.

If we look at our own life in our parish churches and in the wider church, we can see clear evidence of the constant temptation to turn revelation into religion, to turn what God wants us to know and to do into what we make of that knowledge and of those demands.

Religion

Religion has a tendency to justify, in the name of God, everything we do or in which we become involved: democracy; free enterprise; capitalism; acquisition of wealth; piling up possessions; protection of private property; success in any business, political, or entertainment venture; victory in sports; backing of a political party; actions on an international level; victory in war.

Religion makes us anxious not only to justify these activities and ventures and to make them acceptable, but to identify them with *the Christian way* of doing things. From nuclear family to old folks' homes, we consider *our* way not only as the civilized way, but as the *godly* manner of dealing with family, the sick, and the poor. Religion is our own creation. Its horizons are necessarily limited to our horizons. Since it is our creation it will serve us. In a time of social, political, and economic upheaval, we look to it as that one, solid, taken-for-granted basis to our lives. It leads us to cling to the forms and structures with which we are familiar and which we have found comforting. At the dying of an age and the birth of a new one, religion will be in the forefront of those institutions clinging desperately to that immovable rock of unanalyzed assumptions.

But revelation shatters that rock, disturbs our horizons, presents a God who is not like us at all, a destabilizing and surprising God who cannot be used to justify all our projects; instead, One who asks us questions we do not want to hear.

The pre-Vatican II church had settled down into the comfortable position of a religion that had all the answers. The post-Vatican church emerges as a church of the people of God with few answers and many new questions, a pilgrim church in search of the final truth, but never quite arriving there. Yet the signs of religion are still all around us.

The gospel makes clear what the manner and style of leadership in the community of Christ should be like: "You know that among the pagans the rulers lord it over them, and their great men make their authority felt. This is not to happen among you. No, anyone who wants to be great among you must be your servant, and anyone who wants to be first among you must be your slave" (Mt. 20:25–27). Luke adds the detail about titles: "Among pagans . . . those who have authority over them are given the title benefactor. This must not happen with you" (Lk. 27:25–26).

Jesus is recorded several times as warning about titles and terms of dignity: "Why do you call me good? No one is good but God. . . . Call no one father, call no one master." Church history points out very clearly that we have simply and blithely ignored this specific injunction of Scripture (for a variety of justifiable reasons), and have supplanted it with what *we* make of this injunction: "pontifex maximus, his holiness, eminent cardinal, his grace, archbishop, my lord bishop, father"—and all the power and lording it over others implied in such titles. This is one of the clearest examples of turning revelation into religion. Modern popes up until John XXIII did not allow anyone to eat with them, an astonishing interpretation of Jesus of Nazareth, who seemed always to be eating with others.

It is not a radical or impious thing to say that all these things, along with the coat of arms for bishops, the elegantly differentiated colored robes for the hierarchy ("those who wear fine clothes are to be found in palaces"), the attitude of "being born for the purple" of newly appointed bishops (thus separating themselves forever from the ordinary ranks of Christian lay people), do not reflect the mind of Christ and have no basis or echo in the gospel. No one can deny this.

But one has to wonder about the credibility of a church that accepts without qualms all these patently nongospel values, and at the same time argues with the most abstruse reasoning that ordination of women is doctrinally impossible because it is not found in Scripture and is therefore against the mind of Christ and of God.

These nongospel accretions and interpretations, which crept into the church after the time of the Council of Jerusalem, may well have had some meaning and value in the second state of the church—the Gentile, Roman-Hellenic, Mediterranean church. It is difficult to imagine what value they could have in the third stage of the church—the world church, the refounded church of Jesus Christ.

Not every example of growth and development is, of course, evil, but every time it is a case of turning an aspect of revelation into a religious formulation of that revelation, it should be recognized as such. The Lord's Supper is revelation; the Roman Rite Mass is religion. The command to preach the gospel is revelation; the restriction of this power to certain experts is religion. The power conferred on the Christian community to forgive sins is revelation; the ritual for the sacrament of confession or reconciliation is religion. The charism of leadership and administration and presiding over a Christian community, a

charism approved of and discerned by the church, is revelation;
the Roman Catholic priesthood, celibate and male, is religion.
The church as a chosen race, a royal priesthood, a consecrated
nation, and people of God is revelation; the church divided into
clergy and lay people is religion.

A church that reaches far beyond its own boundaries to the
ends of the earth is revelation. A church that is concerned only
with those members who have already come to it is religion. A
church that points to the presence of the Holy Spirit outside its
walls is revelation. A church that condemns everything non-
Christian is religion. A church that stands on the side of the
poor and hungers for justice is revelation. A church that justifies
the possession of great wealth and mollifies its powerful possessors, using God to condone injustice and oppression, is religion—and *bad religion* that distorts the gospel message.

Looking to the liberating meaning and spirit of laws and regulations is revelation. Considering the mere fulfillment of laws
and regulations as holiness and justification, already achieved,
is religion and pharisaism. A human, intelligent, self-sacrificing
obedience is revelation. An obsequious, subservient obedience
is religion, and the closest thing to open revolt.

Praying simply with few words, without feeling the necessity
of informing God of every need at babbling length; trust in divine providence and lack of anxiety about daily needs; lack of
condemnation and judgment and showing a merciful approach
to weak and sinful human beings; a willingness to pay the high
cost of discipleship—these are revelation.

Long, monotonous prayers scheduled by the hour, the longer
and more monotonous the holier they are deemed; worry connected with acquisition of daily needs and success; harsh, condemnatory judgments on others in the name of God; a guarded,
prudent, need-to-keep-up-appearances approach as to how far
to follow Jesus as a disciple—these are religion.

It is not always the clergy and the hierarchy who turn revelation into religion. Christians who look on their church as a
place of refuge or as a sanctuary of personal satisfaction and
fulfillment and comfort, and ignore the meaning of the church
as existing in the world for the nonchurch; who consider the
Eucharist an occasion of personal escape and concern, and for-

get the fact that "every time we break this bread together, we proclaim the death of the Lord" to those who do not know the meaning of that death for their own living and dying; who look at church attendance as a mere satisfaction for legal obligation; who look on the sacraments of baptism of children and matrimony as social requirements without attendant gospel obligations, and penance as a cleansing agent apart from any need for conversion and celebration of God's mercy — all these have done an efficient job of turning revelation into religion.

But most of all those who in the midst of their daily lives and in the midst of their human culture somehow ignore the clear-cut call of Christ to live their lives according to the full dimensions of their faith, to let the gospel message not only fulfill their lives and their culture, but also prophesy against them; to let something in their lives live and something in their culture die — these are people of religion, not of revelation and faith.

Every culture has the peaks and the valleys, the highs and the lows that actually serve as the entrance points for the gospel of Christ. But we can sometimes become so mesmerized by our culture that we can block those entrance points, those very openings through which the gospel is trying to enter into our lives. We can ignore precisely that to which the gospel is speaking in our culture. We can pretend we do not hear it and turn our attention elsewhere to look for salvation and holiness.

As a people we can be burdened with the deepest racial hatred and ethnic blindness and prejudice, and somehow resent the slightest suggestion that the gospel has anything to say about these matters. As a nation we can be prone to the most primitive instinct for violence, armed and otherwise, as a remedy and solution for our fears and insecurities both on behalf of and against our loved ones, and we can turn our minds away and imagine that it is of no concern to our faith life. We can accept blindly the dictates of our culture delineating the meaning of a person solely in terms of his or her productivity; we can come to terms with the insatiable hunger in us for a "part of the American pie and the American dream" honestly or dishonestly acquired — for the possessions, the wealth, the *good life*, success, status, and the equating of all these things with happiness — and pretend that Jesus never said a word about the blessedness of the poor, or the mammon of iniquity, or the impossibility of serving both God and money.

We can submerge all these things in our spiritual consciousness and ask instead, like the rich young man, "What good deed, what good work, what one good action or series of actions can I perform to attain eternal life, to be saved?" And we, like him, can go away sad because we receive no answer to our religious question. We are not willing to trade religion for faith, to pay the terrible cost of discipleship.[2]

We Americans can recognize in the story of the rich young man, in an eerily accurate way, *our* story. He was good and venturesome and generous in spirit. And so are we. He was especially loved by Christ and blessed by God. And so are we. He was rich. So, as a nation, are we. He was invited to walk in the company of Jesus with a personal call, "Come, follow me," to carry out a special mission in the church and in the world. And so, indeed, are we. Will it be our destiny also, like his, to be forever remembered in history as the thirteenth apostle?

7

The Church of the Third Wave

DOCTRINE AND SACRAMENT IN A DESTANDARDIZED CHURCH

The Extraordinary Synod of Rome, 1985, finished its last session with a plea to Pope John Paul II for the compilation of a universal catechism to be used throughout the world. No sooner had the synod closed than a cardinal father of the synod, the one at whose intervention in the synod the idea of a universal catechism was first introduced, announced that he had such a catechism already written and would present it to the pope, asking that it be accepted as the "universal" catechism.[1] The particular congregation he headed had composed it over a period of the five years preceding the Synod of 1985. "It was," he said, "divided into two parts, one doctrinal and one moral." The doctrinal part contained 160 points of doctrine, and the moral part 60 precepts. When asked if this proposed universal catechism would apply everywhere—Africa, Asia, the South Sea islands—he answered that of course it would apply everywhere, that the doctrine of the church is the same everywhere. "The Trinity is the Trinity," he explained, "in the North as well as in the South."[2]

All we would have to do to accept the cardinal's *universal* catechism is to agree that Christianity is simply a set of doctrines, 160 to be exact, and moral precepts, 60 in number. But what if we could not believe that Christianity is a set of doctrines or philosophies or theologies like Hinduism or Buddhism, not a set of morals or laws or commandments as Judaism or Islam might be? What if we believe that Christianity does not have the form of doctrines or moral precepts at all, but has human form, a God-human named Jesus Christ? What if we believed that Christianity is not a doctrine or an ethic, but an event, a history, a story—"once upon a time something happened to this world of ours and to a person who was born, died, and rose on this planet"? If this is what we believe, and the Apostles' Creed testifies to the solidity of this belief, then the cardinal's *universal* catechism would be of no use to us. Nor to anyone.

The Trinity is a glorious example of a concept in a culture reaching to the limits of its powers, and beyond, in expressing a divine truth in such a way that it comprises an ongoing revelation of value to humankind, but especially to that part of humankind that understands the meaning of *personhood* and *nature* and *substance* and *being*. Perhaps the nonbiblical word "Trinity," conveying the concept of three distinct Persons in one divine nature, is not the only way to express the truth we hold when we profess, in that same Apostles' Creed, belief in "the Father, Son and Holy Spirit"—one God. Perhaps there is a way, which we do not yet know, to formulate the same belief in the context of the cultures of Hinduism, Buddhism, and other non-Christian religions or in terms of modern science. If "the Trinity is the Trinity in the North as well as in the South," then other concepts must be the same in the North as well as in the South—such ideas as hypostatic union, transubstantiation, sanctifying grace, or any of the other "160 doctrines of Christianity." Culture blindness is alive and well in the church.

It would be difficult to imagine the bishops of the world accepting the cardinal's handiwork as the universal catechism. But the difficulty lies, in reality, in searching for any universal catechism in this age. Unity has always been a desirable goal, and a necessary one, for Christianity. The desire for uniformity has been a temptation, on and off, from the earliest days of the church. There is nothing sacred or necessary about standardization. It is not a gospel value as unity is. A catechism is a standardized product. So is the thought that Christianity could possibly consist of 160 doctrines and 60 moral precepts. When you think of the meaning of "Catholic," as comprising all the cultures of the world, it would be difficult to imagine that one standardized form of catechesis could possibly serve all the various cultures that are already part of the church, much less the majority of peoples who as yet have nothing to do with Christianity.

What we need in order to carry on the spirit of Vatican Council II is not a new listing of theological and moral doctrines, as we have been doing time after time through the ages, but a serious consideration of the central message of Christianity that must be addressed to our world today—a message that has as one of its main sources the books of the Bible. Why do we Catholics still attribute such a secondary importance to Scripture that we consistently rank other things above it in order of urgency?

For the bishops of the world, at the urging of the Synod of 1985, to concern themselves yet one more time with the same old, tired reformulation of the doctrinal and moral propositions of an exhausted Christianity is to fall into the same pattern missionaries have followed for generations: to preach doctrines and theologies and philosophies and ethics instead of the gospel of Jesus Christ.

Jesus never called anyone to follow a doctrine or a sterile ethic. He spoke about the Father and concern for other human beings. He called people to respond to him as a person and to walk in his company. The person of Jesus lies at the heart of the gospel. We call non-Christian peoples and Christian people to respond to the person of Jesus, not to doctrines and morals. Refounding the Catholic church can be accomplished only in fidelity to the heart of the gospel, to the mind of Christ, to the person of Christ—not to a list of doctrines *about* Christ or the church that bears his name. Realistically, the vitality and vigor of a young church or an old one can rise only to the level of its original call. It will display the enthusiasm and freshness of a personal, eventful, exciting life-altering decision, or carry forever the unmistakable aroma and mustiness of a library or a museum.

To free the sacraments from standardization does not mean to abandon reverence and faithfulness to their gospel meaning.

It is not a call for unbridled abuses. It is merely a focusing on the essentials of each sacrament, not allowing the essentials to be confused with any form the sacrament has taken in any particular past age. The essentials can be reverently preserved at the same time that one deals with the nonessentials in New Testament freedom. The ritual for baptism of the three thousand on the day of Pentecost was obviously different from that of the Ethiopian eunuch by the deacon Philip, near the stream their carriage passed that day; and different again from the baptism of the jailer and his family by Paul after a night of instruction in the faith.

The three thousand were cut to the heart by Peter's preaching and wanted to know what they must now do. The eunuch had a Bible, belief in the Word spoken by Philip, and saw water in the stream. What was to prevent him from being baptized? The jailer and his family experienced communal conversion. These were the essentials. Who would question the reverence with which they were carried out, despite the undoubted differences between the dramatic spectacle of the christening of the three thousand and the less than stunning ritual of the night baptism of the jailer's family?

The manner of breaking bread certainly and historically differed with each apostle, and was not the same as the way it was done in the house churches of Corinth or in the restrained atmosphere of Jerusalem.

The anointing of the sick performed by the disciples sent out, two by two, by Jesus, grew naturally into the anointing by elders in the time of James. But standardized ritual was hardly a consideration or possibility.

Liturgical regulations were never meant to dominate the meaning of a sacrament or to suppress it entirely. They sometimes did. It is revealing to follow the development of a sacrament from its inception as a gospel value to standardized, full-blown rite.

A constantly recurring theme of the New Testament is forgiveness. It lies at the heart of the Good News to be preached to all the nations of the world. It haunts the pages of the New Testament, and is possibly best captured in essence in the story of the prodigal son and the forgiving father. It is not a story of examination of conscience, of confessing sins by name, of integrity of confession, of mortal sins and venial sins, of absolution, or of satisfaction made for sins. It is a story of forgiveness and celebration and coming back to life again.

But the demand for the standardization of the sacrament of penance, or "reconciliation" in modern times, has taken the joy out of the good news of forgiveness. Worse, it has led to the deprivation of the reception of the sign of forgiveness of the church for untold multitudes of people who desperately need that sign of forgiveness. If there is anything clear in the post-Vatican II church, it is that the people have rejected the sacrament of penance and reconciliation, and church authorities profess to show no alarm.

We carry on as though the relationship with God were the only area in life in which visible signs are not necessary. Signs of forgiveness are necessary, we reason, in love affairs, in friendships, in marriages, in family life, in parent-child and even race relationships—but not in our life with God. We would be alarmed if signs of forgiveness somehow disappeared in all these human relationships. We would come to the conclusion, as missionaries who have worked in foreign cultures realize, that the sign is as real as the thing signified; that if there were no signs of forgiveness in all these personal relationships, there would indeed be no forgiveness at all.

A vast number of Catholics today wander about in their life of faith receiving no sign of forgiveness in their conscience, no sign from their faith community, their church—and none from God. Where there is no sign, there is no forgiveness. Such people carry a heavy burden of guilt. And when they do choose to continue active membership in the church, they often participate with a profound sense of unworthiness and doubt. If one carries this doubt into sacred areas such as Eucharistic and sacramental participation, the sense of unworthiness increases and so does the doubt, leading to a decrease of faith in the sacredness of things being handled.

All kinds of studies have been made researching the history of the sacrament of penance. All the evidence uncovered witnesses to the fact that the standardized version of the sacrament with which we are familiar, and which the overwhelming majority of Catholics find disturbing, is of recent invention as far as the history of the church goes. Still most bishops and modern sacramentalists agree to a mere cosmetic change in the administering of the sacrament and cling tenaciously to the more odious elements of the ritual, such as integral confession of number and kinds of sins, as prescribed by the Council of Trent. The reasoning seems to be that if a relaxation in the rules of conferring the sacrament is suggested, it cannot be permitted. But if a more rigorous interpretation concerning the sacrament has ever been prescribed in history, that stricter interpretation must stand as of divine law. Such has not always been the case in the centuries of the church's life, however.

It is not clear that Christ or the apostles ever envisioned the eventuality of the need for a second repentance toward conversion after the *metanoia* required for baptism. Even the famous words of Christ, as recorded in John, about "whose sins you shall forgive" most probably referred to the sins of non-Christians *before* baptism, not of Christians *after* baptism.

St. Paul seems to think that some sins do revoke the conversion that was necessary at baptism. For certain sins in the Christian communities, Paul acts as if excommunication were the only solution, with community forgiveness clearly impossible, and the fate of the sinners left to the mercy of God.[3] A further forgiveness after baptism was not even allowed in the early church, and when after some years it eventually was allowed, the person receiving it was granted just one more forgiveness in a lifetime. That dispensation, as meager as it seems, was at least a relaxation of a sterner discipline.

Further relaxation was to come centuries later. That *second forgiveness* had to be asked for and received publicly, with all the humiliation and demeaning penance that was involved. This dispiriting process continued for centuries. The further relaxation took place in the sixth century, when the begging for second forgiveness (hitherto a public request) could be carried out privately. It probably seemed a terrible concession to laxity at the time. More *laxity* crept in when that second forgiveness grew into a third and a fourth and even more forgivenesses.

The next emphasis in the church was the aspect of *satisfaction* for sins, to make up for the public penances that had accompanied public confession. It reigned dominant until the twelfth century, when *absolution* for sins (an idea that had not been emphasized for a thousand years) suddenly became a necessity and, in fact, the essence of the sacrament. In the thirteenth century, private confession became a law. What was formerly forbidden was now commanded.

In the sixteenth century, the Council of Trent decreed that integral confession of sins by name, number, and kind (mortal and venial sins being clearly distinguished), and the imparting of absolution by ordained priests alone, were essentially and positively required—not just by church law but "by divine law."[4]

After such an extraordinary, jumbled history, with no clearly discernible pattern of development, and filled with huge lapses and apparently contradictory emphases in different eras of that history, it is difficult to understand Trent's insistence on divine law as the source of its many prescriptions concerning the sacrament of penance. Perhaps a little honesty and humility would have been more fitting. No other doctrine in the church, moral or dogmatic, after such a checkered, disjointed history, would ever have similar claims of divine origin made for it. It leaves entire centuries outside the possibility of valid reception of the sacrament of penance—including our own.

Every age has exercised the right to adapt and interpret the sacrament according to the needs of the time, keeping faithful, as far as possible, to the essential meaning of forgiveness as it appears in the New Testament. Is our age the only age that does not have this right? Are we alone forever trapped by the laws of the past, even when these laws themselves do not follow a consistent pattern?

Indeed, since Vatican Council II there has been an effort to renew the sacrament of reconciliation, to adapt it to our age and to a deeper understanding of the sacrament. Remarkable steps have been taken along that line in pointing out that conversion is of the essence of New Testament forgiveness, an essential element that has too long been neglected, and that sinfulness, not individual acts of sin, and God's mercy, not condemnation of sinners, lie at the heart of the sacrament. But having gone this far, the New Rite stops at the wall of Trent, and refuses to go beyond the necessity of integral confession of names and kinds and numbers of sins and judicial absolution. No matter what attractive new aspects it brings to the ritual of confession, such as face-to-face dealing with the confessor, communal penance ceremonies, and general absolution, it returns in each case to the boundaries set by Trent, and thus leaves the sacrament basically where it has been for the last four hundred years, and leaves church leaders wondering why the new ritual has not attracted Christians by the thousands and thousands to return to the confessional.

If the church could move from no possibility at all of further forgiveness after baptism to a single, once-in-a-lifetime second opportunity of forgiveness, public though it had to be; to a possibility of private forgiveness, many times repeated; to an emphasis on absolution rather than satisfaction; to a requirement for annual private confession; to a necessity of integral confession of mortal sins and sacerdotal absolution — could it not move even beyond that for the sake of the forgiveness that haunts the pages of the New Testament?

In the community of Christ that has become the world church, in the refounded church, in the church of the Third Wave, should we not begin a destandardized approach to the sacrament, taking in all the values of preceding ages and moving beyond them to what we see has been a neglected and immeasurable value and restore it to the church? We should not do this in a spirit of confrontation and bitterness, but simply and quietly through a realization that we have an essential ministerial responsibility to carry out to the best of our ability. The first private confessions and sacramental acts of forgiveness that were carried out were done so against the ecclesiastical legislation of the day out of pastoral concern and necessity. Through compassionate use they became the law of the church that we know today. We have like needs today and just as urgent a necessity to dispense forgiveness to our world. Not out of lack of respect but, rather, out of deep reverence for the sacrament of penance and for the sake of carrying out the purpose of the New Rite, we have to try to effect the deeper understanding of conversion and forgiveness and celebration that the New Rite uncovers, an understanding that goes far beyond the faltering, incomplete efforts of Trent. Is it irreverent to suggest that we today have an opportunity to understand better the meaning of New Testament forgiveness than the hassled fathers of Trent in the midst of an ecclesiastical revolution? Isn't it possible that we could move beyond Trent to such an extent that what is not allowed today could become the church practice of tomorrow, a kind of destandardized ritual?

Conversion would be the dominant idea. Conversion is not a weekly experience. It is a lifelong process often marked by distinct experiences in different stages of life. Devotional confessions would recede and disappear. Their place could be taken by other means of spiritual direction. Confession would occur at stages of conversion or necessary renewal in life, or after serious deviation from baptismal promises. Eucharist would once again be looked at as the ordinary means of forgiveness for "the just man and woman who fall seven times daily." The sacrament of reconciliation would not be conferred at all where there is no conversion, either initial or continuing. The matter of the sacrament would not be sinful acts, which are often nothing more than the opportunity for sin to be worked out in practice—such as racist acts or words having actually been carried out because the aggravating occasion arose—but, rather, deep-seated sins, such as a racism that may or may not have had the opportunity to be vented. According to the teachings of Jesus, a person is not an adulterer just when one has the opportunity to be.

Those sinful acts, or opportunities of sinfulness actually being carried out according to kind, name, and number, would not be the requisite for confession. But the sinfulness itself would be, whether it is racism, hatred, cruelty, essential self-centeredness, the constant consideration of others as objects of sexual gratification, or devastating pride. It is often the "unknown" sins or unacknowledged sins, a sinfulness perhaps recognized by everyone else but the sinner, that are the often entirely neglected proper material for confession, a neglect that can endure for a lifetime. All this has nothing to do with temptation. Temptation is not sinfulness. Jesus was tempted in everything as we are.

The singular benefit or grace of this sacramental encounter would not be so much the sacerdotal absolution, but the sign of forgiveness—humanly needed, eagerly sought, and gratefully received—a sign given by the Christian community, a sign that is as real as the thing it signifies, namely, that forgiveness has touched the earth and that weak and fallible human beings can always begin anew, and that no one has to be a failure forever.

I have dwelt on the sacrament of reconciliation at some length because it is a clear example of a sacrament having fallen in terrible misuse, being rejected by and large, in its present state, by an overwhelming majority of the faithful—with neither its perennial misuse nor its rejection being acknowledged or recognized by the official church. To include such a sacrament, so poorly understood and practiced, in the liturgical celebration of the Good News of Jesus Christ, and to expect it to be accepted as such by the as yet unevangelized peoples of the world, shows a poor understanding of the missionary problem today. What is not fit for home consumption should not be exported to the non-Christian nations of the world. Penance is only one of the sacraments that stands in desperate need of destandardization.

How long shall we wait before we admit that the idea for a male, celibate, seminary-trained, rigidly standardized (according to Western ideals) priesthood will not make it in the world in which the church is situated today? Until our seminaries are completely empty? Until our dioceses are staffed by just half the personnel necessary for ministry on the most minimal level? (At the present rate of decrease this will take place within a decade of this writing.) Or shall we wait until the priest–lay-Christian ratio approaches that of South America?

No organization or society is deliberately self-destructive or suicidal. It will not purposely refuse to take the steps necessary to ensure its continued existence. The church community will find a way of providing ministry and ministers for itself and for its members. It always has. It always will. It would be a blessing if it would do so while it still has the opportunity of responding freely to the most beautiful meaning of the New Testament rather than to an emergency situation of leaderless flocks.

A DESPECIALIZED CHURCH

There has always been a temptation in the church to seek positions of honor and power. It started with the companions of

Jesus. The mother of James and John asked that Jesus give place of highest privilege to her sons, one at the right hand, the other at the left, in the kingdom (Mt. 20:20–22). Jesus discovered the apostles arguing several times as to who should be first among them (Mk. 9:33–34; 10:41). The tendency to seek distinction and division of power entered the church at an early stage. Clement of Rome and Ignatius of Antioch staked claims for bishops and priests and deacons as privileged holders of power.[5] The process continued and intensified throughout church history. But only in modern, industrialized times has the desire for exclusive expertise, known as specialization, become a passion in the church.

This expertise extends to every facet of church leadership and has an ominous quality of exclusivity attached to it. All specialization does. It was expressed in its most blatant form by Pope Gregory XVI (1831–46): "No one can deny that the church is an unequal society in which God destined some to be governors and others to be servants. The latter are the laity; the former the clergy."[6] Pope Pius X was equally ominous: "Only the college of pastors has the right and authority to lead and govern. The masses have no right or authority except that of being governed, like an obedient flock that follows its shepherd."[7]

The exclusivity of specialization in the church reaches far and wide and deep. It divides the church into the specialists and the privileged, on one side, and the "ordinary underprivileged," on the other. It is so all-pervasive that we have come to accept it as the normal and unchangeable face of the church. It is difficult to think of the church in any other — despecialized — way.

Every Sunday we recite in the ancient creed: "We believe in *one, holy, catholic, apostolic* church," basing our belief on the essential marks or notes of the true church. The church of Christ would have to include these qualities. But the qualities themselves become the exclusive possession of the specialists.

One: Unity is achieved by the idea of one doctrinal formulation or one theology, which is the province of the doctrinal specialists, who become so either by office or by acceptance as such by those in office. Left out of this unity are the representatives of differing theologies stemming from different cultures. Also left out are the vast majority of ordinary Christians, who are not specialists and who are viewed as having no right to theologize. The community of Christ must preserve the unity of the gospel message, but the Word of God was never meant just for specialists. It is for all. This unity is also conceived of as being accomplished by the use of just one liturgy, ignoring the countless possibilities of cultural differences in liturgical expression—the cultural expression of very ordinary, untrained people. Unity of a kind is also effectively brought about by a single canon law for the entire world, the specialty of Western canonists. What is thus achieved, of course, is Western uniformity, not world unity.

Holy: Holiness has long been the prerogative of the clerical and religious specialists. The canonized saints have always been priests and religious, together with those few lay people who have successfully imitated clerical and religious spirituality. Surely holiness is not for specialists, but for all followers of Christ. Yet there is probably not another example in the whole of church life that so clearly shows such a restricting of an important Christian value to a minority group as the idea of sanctity. Lay people would be hard pressed to describe a unique and distinct lay spirituality, one without all the tell-tale marks of the monastery and rectory—one filled instead with the earthy flavor of human life.

Catholic: A community is not catholic when a single form or structure of church and hierarchy and ministry and sacraments is imposed indiscriminately across the world. This is a system that reaches the whole world but is not open to the whole world. The modern world is made up of many cultures that are foreign to the sending church, including the growing planetary culture of science and technology. To be catholic is to be incarnated in each of these cultures in such a way that the very face of the church will be changed. The agents of such a change could not be specialists within the church, but necessarily must be people outside the church, in dialogue with the community of Christ.

Apostolic: The claim for apostolicity in the church is a clear example of specialization. It is based on the concept of apostolic power being passed from the original twelve apostles, perhaps by a physical chain of hands across the centuries, to those appointed bishops in the church today. And that apostolicity resides in, and is guaranteed by, those bishops alone. But do we really see such meticulous care being taken in the New Testament to ensure that direct connection with the original apostles? What do we know about Andrew or Philip or Nathanael or Matthew or the other James or Judas or Simon the freedom fighter? Did they ever impose hands on anyone? And what of Paul? Was he not an apostle quite separate from the twelve? And Barnabas and Apollos? In the Epistle to the Romans, Paul refers to those "outstanding apostles, Andronicus and Junias" (Rom. 16:7). An apostle is "one who is sent to proclaim the good news about the bright future of history, already won by the Resurrection."[8] Is apostolicity a specialty of bishops alone, who may or may not be involved in the proclaiming of this Good News to the world? Is it a static quality inherent in any bishop, whether he be an active proclaimer of the gospel or merely the director of the Vatican Library? Is not apostolicity the quality of a church that is necessarily missionary? Do we not all, as members of the church, share in that apostolicity inasmuch as we are all sent to proclaim the Good News about the bright future of history? Apostolicity does not belong to specialists. The mission of the church is not entrusted to a few. It is given to all.

Peter, the one apostle who might have been tempted to opt for a division of privileges in the church, does not view the church as a community dominated by specialists:

> But you are a chosen race, a royal priesthood, a consecrated nation, a people set apart to sing the praises of God who called you out of darkness into his wonderful light. Once you were not a people at all and now you are the People of God; once you were outside the mercy and now you have been given mercy [1 Pet. 2:9–10].

It is sad that this passage, which clearly visualizes the church as a unified community possessing the sacred power of priesthood, election, consecrated holiness, and mission, should be used as a means of breaking up and dividing the community into the privileged and nonprivileged in the church.

The *people of God* — the *laos theou* — whom Peter mentions become the basis for the *laity*, the disfranchised described by Gregory XVI and Pius X. The separation into clergy and laity begins the division into people with rights and power and authority and those without; into the people who teach the truth, produce holiness, determine the only acceptable form of the church, and possess the apostolic power, and those who merely learn, receive the holiness dispensed, live within the predetermined structure, and submit to the power.

Surely, in faithfulness to the New Testament, it is the other way around. Bishops, priests, and religious are only part of the laity, the *laos theou*, the people of God. The power, authority, and mission they possess do not originate with the people, but come from the Spirit of God, the Spirit of Christ, who has founded and endowed that believing community, making it the one, holy, catholic, and apostolic church.

A DECENTRALIZED CHURCH

St. Paul wrote letters to the church in Rome, to "God's beloved in Rome," to the church of God in Corinth, to the "saints who are at Ephesus," to "you people at Philippi, like no other church," to the saints in Colossae, and to the church in Thessalonica. At different times, he sent various greetings to the deaconess of the church of Cenchreae, to the church that met in the house of Prisca and Aquila, to the whole church that met in the house of Gaius, to the church of the Laodiceans, and to the churches that met in the houses of Nympha and Philemon. Finally, he mentions the churches in Galatia, the churches in Asia, and "all the churches" that sent greetings to the church of Rome.

Paul believed in the one church of Christ, as he believed in "one Lord, one faith, one baptism." But for him the reality of the church, the New Testament presence of the risen Christ that his beloved Christians would experience, was the local church, not some superchurch. Even when he spoke of the church spread out over a vast area, he spoke of it in the plural. He did not speak of the *church* in Asia or the *church* in Galatia or the *world church* that sent its greetings to the church of Rome, but rather, he called them the *churches* of Asia, the *churches* of Galatia, and *all the churches* that greeted Rome.

I do not think he would know what we mean by the church

of Europe, the church of North America or of South America, or the Roman Catholic Church of Christendom. And I do not think he would consider that the unity of the church of Christ would be threatened by the existence or the reemergence of the reality of local churches. Vatican Council II spoke of "the new, the young and the particular churches" of the third world. It underlined the validity of such a concept for our time.

Paul went even further, of course, when he spoke of the churches that met in the houses of Prisca and Aquila and Gaius and Philemon. He could not have been speaking of groups that numbered much more than fifty people in a church community.[9] That might seem strange to us, and yet we know the lack of sense of community people feel with the idea of membership in a monolithic, world superchurch, or even in a national church or in a diocesan church. If truth were told, there is sometimes no experience of community in the most vibrant-appearing, teeming suburban parish churches of America. Where is it that Christian people will experience the reality of the New Testament event in their lives? Wherever it is, *that* is church.

This experience of community on a very local level in no way militates against a profound sense and need of unity with others, whether Christian or non-Christian, outside of the community. In fact, if a Christian community truly understands itself, and the gospel message that calls it into existence, it will be more ready to extend itself to the wider community and the world. An organization or a clan or a tribe or a racial group is mutually exclusive with others of a like nature. A community is not. It is by nature open to other differing or wiser communities.

The local church communities of St. Paul's time did not feel themselves cut off from other, distant communities of Christ. They felt, rather, deeply drawn to union with them, and the warm affection and concern they had for them is outstanding and evident.

We are faced with the necessity of refounding the church of Christ for our age. That does not mean a great many minor changes on the same level at which we have been operating in the church. It means, instead, being faithful to the mind of Christ, and moving to an entirely different level of life and activity in the church. If, indeed, we are entering upon the third stage in the history of the church, the world stage; if the transition from the previous historical and theological situation is to an entirely new one, and the transition is radical enough and decisive enough to constitute a cultural, historical, theological break with the past—then we must go far beyond what recent centuries have ventured to propose in their intramural and intracultural concerns with the church. What we are facing is not merely an intracultural difficulty within the church, but a challenge from all the cultures of the world outside the church. We have to make possible the New Testament life and reality of those "new and young and particular churches" of Vatican II. Such a reality cannot come to be in a severely centralized church.

Even in the older churches, like the churches in America, a new surge of New Testament life is scarcely conceivable when all authority and responsibility for growth, living, action, worship, evangelization, and change must come from far, far above. What we often have instead is organized, controlled stagnation. And it might well be that the churches in America are not the most painful examples of this stagnation existing today.

Today we have to go far back, not to the Middle Ages, but to New Testament times, to the first stage of the church, in which the Christ event took place, "to launch out into the deep," as Jesus commanded, to find the model, the inspiration, the Spirit that will help us refound the Catholic church. The sacred tradition of the ages will guide and enlighten our journey as searchers in the pilgrim church, even if that journey takes us far from the center, far from the Vatican, away from the chancery, away from the sacristy and sanctuary of the parish church into the neighborhoods where people dwell and toil and play and marry and die—even if it leads us finally to churches as far distant and different as the ones that met in the houses of Philemon and Prisca and Aquila. And there is nothing to prevent "all these churches" from continuing to send their greetings to the church in Rome.

8

Heirs of the World

THE CHURCH IN THE MIDST OF CREATION

Pitirim Sorokin spoke of our being at the beginning of a coming Ideational culture of a creative tomorrow, involving the whole way of life and thought and conduct of Western society and civilization. This spiritual, unified system of thought, based on a simple, single principle, will determine the future age, a time when science and technology, the undisputed masters of / the previous age, will serve and cooperate with that guiding spiritual principle. Many observers of this dawning age of humankind differ as to exact descriptions of its makeup and essential structure, but not one of them disagrees concerning the arena in which this new age will work its way out. No one doubts that it will indeed be the entire globe, the planet earth, the world. That is why Karl Rahner's insight into the fundamental theological interpretation of Vatican Council II is so significant, that the area in which the church must now find its meaning and live out its life is indeed, for the first time, the entire world. We can no longer think of anything less than the world.

It is sad and ironic that at present two views of the world are bitterly vying for attention and dominance: the religious view, and the secular, scientific view. The religious view, by and large, is still involved with the saving and redeeming of a fallen, sinful world, while the scientific view is focused on the creation of a new world. The interest of this latter focus is evidenced in the very terminology it uses to describe the origin of the world: the fiery outburst of creation, the "big bang" of creation. The energies of the churches are too often consumed in fighting and condemning sin and saving people from the clutches of pornography and the sexual revolution.[1]

The scientific community has appropriated our Christian vision, and we have not even noticed the appropriation or borrowing of that vision. It is we who originally believed in the new creation, already begun on this planet earth with the resurrection.

Many official religious pronouncements, coming forth from the Vatican and the centers of other mainline churches, or from the electronic television churches, or from devout Islamic nations, are condemnatory and obsessed with sin and the fallen human race. Our religious preoccupation is directed to saving and redeeming a flawed world.

We must move away from a theology of salvation and redemption to a theology of creation, or at least come to the realization that the holy way of salvation is indeed the same thing as the continuing process of creation; that the saving God is the same as the God of creation—that creation and salvation are one thing. To separate them and to concentrate only on saving and redeeming the world is to deny creation. We are not destined to be saved *from* this world, but *in* this world.

We believe in a sacred world, going somewhere, under the guidance of the Creator. It has already come a long way. It is, in our faith, like the Eucharistic bread that we handle, which began as a tiny seed with all the power of creation within it. It was planted by human hands and nurtured, watered, and harvested with human care, and then the grains of wheat were ground into flour and baked into bread with human skill. And as we handle it with faith we believe that, through human intention and human word, the bread has a long way to go, destined as it is to become the body of Christ. And so it is with the earth and with the world. They, too, have a long way to go—destined, through divine power and human intervention, to become the body of Christ.

The heart of the whole biblical message is a call to break out of the endless, relentless turning wheel of the pagan world, where every tomorrow will be like today, as predictable and inescapable as the rhythm of the daily and monthly and yearly cycle of the earth. The biblical message breaks that unending fateful cycle of human life with the eruption of the messianic promise bursting on the world. This is the vision of the Jewish prophets. The kingdom of God, so beloved of Jesus of Nazareth, is a message of hope, not an apocalyptic judgment on the world. It is a gospel of the new creation, of the world becoming what God always meant it to be.

The scientific world has stolen our messianic vision. It is no longer dominated by the terrible "single vision" of Francis Bacon and Isaac Newton. It has responded to the plea of William Blake:

> And twofold Always, May God us keep
> From Single Vision & Newton's sleep![2]

The single vision of Newton, as poet William Blake conceived of it, was the deliberate attempt to purify reality of all superstition, to keep it just as it appeared to be: that which could be seen and heard and measured and weighed and counted. It was a cleansing of reality of all that was sacred, magical, mysterious, transcendent and sacramental. Science provided the ultimate and only truth—the single vision. Whatever science could accomplish in quest of that truth, it should be allowed to pursue.

Some people considered William Blake mad, but perhaps it takes a certain kind of poetic madness to call attention to the terrible danger lying in such a view of truth and of the world. Perhaps "sleep" or "trance" is the best word to describe the state of consciousness of a scientific-technological culture that would lead us to the brink of a poisoned earth and atmosphere and seascape, and thermonuclear destruction.

Science has moved beyond this narrow destructive view and has already stepped into the new Ideational age so aptly described by Sorokin. It is no longer dictated to merely by measurements, data, engineering, and agricultural miracles. It is beginning to be guided by a new vision looking to the entire earth and all humankind, to the full human dimension, including those aspects that cannot be seen and mathematically measured. If a new, simple idea or principle is emerging, it is no longer the *single*, uniform vision of Newton, but a universal vision that encompasses all reality in a masterful unity.

What is happening now is the greatest transformation of life and consciousness that has taken place since the rise of the greater civilizations, which Sorokin would describe as the first Ideational age in history.[3] Religious thought as we know it today, even Christian thought, is not broad enough, or earthwide enough, or catholic enough to respond to the convulsive reality of the present age. And yet, the Christian vision cannot be less than that of the non-Christian and scientific world that it must evangelize. We have long since reached the time for a wider ecumenism, the true ecumenism.

It is time to let the Christ grow into the dimensions of the cosmic Christ. It is not foreign to Christian thought to conceive of the human being in relation to that Christ:

> He has let us know the mystery of his purpose, the hidden plan he so kindly made in Christ from the beginning . . . that he would bring everything together under Christ, as head, everything in the heavens and everything on earth. . . . He has put all things under his feet, and made him, as the ruler of everything, the head of the church, which is his body, the fullness of him who fills the whole creation [Eph. 1:9–10, 22–23].

Paul leads his readers gently to the full dimensions of his belief: "If you read my words, you will have some idea of the depths that I see in the mystery of Christ" (Eph. 3:4), and to its implications for human beings themselves: "In this way we are all to come to unity in our faith and in our knowledge of the Son of God, until we become the perfect Man, fully mature with the fullness of Christ himself" (Eph. 4:13). We ourselves are to come to age, to grow in the dimensions of the cosmic Christ, until we become, as Paul says, the perfect person. Paul's new person is not an individual, but is clearly nothing else than the new humanity, a Christian ideal that is not really inimical to Buddhism or science or capitalism or Marxism.

Our growing consciousness, both as Christians and as humans, of our common bond with humankind, and our relationship to the whole earth, is a dramatic change in our appreciation of the Christian message and of the church. Just as we now are naturally conscious of being in space, so are we just as aware of the belief that Christianity must relate to the entire world in a way that we did not know before. It is really a matter of a further and decisive awakening of Christianity, a kind of revelation.

There are convincing reasons to believe that we are entering into the greatest period of change the world has ever known, that the time has come to dream of a new earth.[4] A Christianity lived apart from all this would soon have no meaning. A vast change is taking place in the entire human order.[5] The religious awareness needed at this time will have to be of a kind that we have never known before.

EVANGELIZATION IN THE NEW AGE

Whatever we call this new age—be it the World Stage of the church, or the Ideational age, or the Third Wave, or the Ecological age—we cannot abandon evangelization for this age. Evangelization means bringing the gospel to bear upon culture—all culture. The notion and meaning of culture is one of the most important discoveries and revelations of our time. Whether in the business world, the world of industry, of education, of politics and government—or the world of religion—culture is one of the most necessary determining factors in any endeavor undertaken. It permeates every aspect of human life and human striving. It affects every single thing in which a person becomes involved. It is that second, artificial layer of reality that is added on to the first, natural layer and level of human existence.[6] A stream is nature; a canal is culture. A grunt is nature; a word is culture. Sex is nature; marriage is culture. There would be no understanding of religion at all outside culture. In the process of evangelization, culture makes the gospel understandable, and dialogue possible. That is what evangelization is—dialogue—and it is absolutely essential for our age. Evangelization is not proselytism or brain-washing or propagandizing or even convert-making. It is dialogue and there are two necessary components of this dialogue for us: authentic gospel, and a true openness to conversion.[7]

In any dialogue in which we might become involved, we have

to bring the full brunt of the Christian gospel to bear on the culture facing us. The whole notion of Christ, both as the Jesus of the Gospels and as the cosmic Christ of St. Paul, is essential to our sharing in the phenomenon of this present earthwide awareness. It will be of no value if we bring a watered-down version of the gospel with us, in the mistaken belief that a weakened version may be more acceptable.

When we enter this dialogue with all the cultures of the world or with the milieu of science and technology, we must be open to conversion—conversion to a fuller truth. If we are not open to conversion, then the process we are involved in is not one of evangelization but of proselytism. If we are not open to conversion, then we have no right to enter into true religious dialogue.

Only a dialogue with such cultures opens us to the proper sphere of Christianity and the church—the earth and the world. And only in this sphere can we really come to an understanding of Christianity that will speak to this age. Familiar concepts take on new, deeper significance, as we reach out to all humankind and all the earth. The words of Jesus "to preach the Gospel to all creation" open up a vision of the earth redeemed and renewed as "the pearl of great price" and the godly kingdom. And what of those who cast aside their arrogance toward other human beings and cultures and religions and are gentle and humble enough to be open to conversion? Are they not the ones "who shall inherit the earth"?

Dialogue with the scientific culture will remind us of our own gospel belief in the sacredness of the earth. Should anyone be more zealously aware than a Christian of the urgency of the question of life and death of the planet earth itself? Why would we ever consider such ground as foreign or strange to Christians, or somehow unreligious? The scientific world needs to be reminded again and again of the presence of the divine and the sacred in the midst of the world of things, which its practitioners handle with such self-assurance. "This *[all this]* is my body"— the body of God. This sacramental vision is a necessary safeguard against a totally desanctified world, a world devoid of mystery and transcendence—against the terrible single vision of Isaac Newton.

Dialogue is no longer a luxury. It is a necessity in the world of today. No community or body on the earth possesses absolute truth or the answer to the earth-threatening problems facing humankind.[8] We must begin to look on others as "others possessing truth," so that their truth might become ours, that we all might move out of the isolation in which we have been operating.

As we look back now we realize that the Catholic world was in an exhausted and deteriorating state in the period immediately preceding Vatican Council II. We cannot even imagine today what might have happened to the church if there had been no Vatican Council II. There were many outward signs of strength and beauty, with seminaries and religious life burgeoning, Catholic schools at every level, and Sunday church attendance at an all-time high. But insularity was growing apace with numbers, and the church was becoming more and more cut off from the modern world, having less and less effect on the world, with the gospel message being buried among the laws and doctrines and otherworldly spirituality of a standardized and centralized church. Abuse of spiritual power in religious life, parish life, and diocesan life reached levels that are difficult to believe today. The drying up of gospel life and vitality, the process of deteriorization and exhaustion had set in a long time before Vatican II.

The same seems to be true for all the other Christian churches. We are not as different as we like to believe. Vatican Council II was an important milestone for them also, a prophetic event, and, though few may have yet acknowledged it, it was also a watershed for Islam and Buddhism and Hinduism. These great religions also have been in a process of stagnation for a long time.[9] The growth of the scientific-technological culture across the world has been even more of a threat to them than to Christianity. They, too, are experiencing convulsive change. They are entering into radically new situations and are beginning to view themselves differently. Political demonstrations, self-immolations, protests, activism of Buddhist and Hindu monks and priests — all are basic departures from their own previous understanding of the world and their part in it.

Kairos is a special moment in time filled with meaning and calling for action. When that special moment arrives, we have to rise to it, respond to it, or that moment can be lost forever. Jesus knew when his hour had come and he rose to it. There have been missionary moments like that in the history of the church, some responded to, some lost for the ages. There is such a moment now. The *kairos* of our time is the meeting of all the religious traditions in the world in their movement toward affirming that spirituality is concerned with the entirety of human experience.[10] Liberation theologians are not the only ones awaking from the deep sleep of false spirituality.

The world of Islam is in the same turmoil that grips other religions. The fanatical suicide bombers and holy-war raiders are striving desperately to return to a past that is forever lost, refusing to admit that Islam has gone through the same stages of decay and exhaustion as Christianity. It is impossible to recapture that lost glory, because to do so they have to deny the whole modern world.

If only there were dialogue among the great religions, we might to able to point out to them the one thing we have found out with certainty about the direction any religion will take today. It cannot go backward. It cannot return to the past. It must go forward to the future, whatever pain and uncertainty that future may hold. We could share with them the tension and the struggle in any religious body divided over just how progressively or how conservatively a religion should move — with good people on both sides of the struggle.

The worlds of Islam and Buddhism and other religions, in their isolated positions, have reached the end of their inner possibilities and growth. That Catholic Christianity which today has the same dimension as European and American Christianity has reached the same state. We have come to the end of that Catholicism, a Catholicism so isolated from the rest of the world. And perhaps we have come to an end of isolated Christianity. It has nothing more to say.

The religions and faiths of the world have to enter into dialogue with each other and with the scientific culture. All must bring the full and authentic messages of their tradition with them. A fanatical and distorted Islam will be of no more use than a narrow, partial, watered-down or distorted Christianity. Only the full and complete Christianity can speak with an equally complete Islam or Hinduism in any authentic dialogue leading to the unity of spiritual understanding necessary for the future of our planet earth.

As Christians, we believe that the Holy Spirit is still working always and everywhere, unpredictably and outside the boundaries that *we* have set. The Spirit sets no boundaries, as much to our surprise as it was to the early Jewish Christians, who saw the Spirit poured out on Gentiles, beyond the limits that reasonable religious people had expected. The ancestors of those Jewish Christians had made an exodus out of the slavery of Egypt. What was required of them now was a second exodus, just as daring as the first. They never made it.[11]

An exodus is required of us at this time: an exodus from the Sensate age into the Ideational; from the industrial era into the new Third Wave; from the technological into the ecological age; from a church of Europe and America into the church of the world. The church must be evangelized by the world. Christianity must be studied, not from inside out, but from outside inward. Christians, until the present time, have not distinguished themselves in their concern for the destiny of the earth. It will be the sacred task of this generation of the followers of Christ to fill this terrible lack. If we believe, and we do, that God had desired to become a member of the earth community, then we can do no less.

A NEW EARTH

In speaking of dialogue and openness to conversion, we can conceive of such things easily enough in relation to the other great religions of the world, but we might have some difficulty with the thought of evangelization of the scientific-technological culture that is covering the world. Such a culture has always been considered the enemy of all religions and the seducer and destroyer of faith. What do we have in common with science and technology? What possibility of dialogue? To what conversion could we be called by such a culture? What revelation could conceivably lie in its midst?[12]

Evangelization is always a matter of mutual fecundation and interpenetration, a search for common ground and common language to make dialogue possible. The common ground here is *creation*. Evangelization is a movement outward from the center toward the culture being evangelized. It is for us to accept the basic scientific concept of creation as a truth possessed by that culture, as a revelation, as common ground, as common language with which to begin the dialogue and the conversion to a fuller truth. The origin of the universe as scientifically conceived can be our common language. The unique cosmic emergence of the universe from a central fiery outburst does no violence to our idea of creation. Indeed, the idea of the entire universe in its present state having come forth from that tiny original particle and "big bang" of creation is satisfyingly consonant with our biblical idea of the continuing process of creation. Such a view is the basis of the scientific image of the universe and is the heart of the biblical image. God, creator of the world, is also maker of the laws that govern it, according to the Bible, which necessitates creative powers being active every moment. Faith in the creative power of God was of the essence of the religion of Israel. Genesis expounded that faith in narrative form—"And God said, 'Let there be light.'" Job expressed it in poetry, including the only verse in the Bible that hints at infinite space:

> He it was who spread the North above the void,
> And poised the earth on nothingness [Job 26:7].

According to both the scientific and biblical views, the process of creation is not over. It is continuing into the new creation. The men and women of science are dreaming of a new earth and a new humankind, a new quality of human life from birth to grave. And so do we believe, we people of the Bible: "For now I create new heavens and a new earth. . . . No more will be found the infant living a few days only, or the old man not living to the end of his days" (Is. 65:17–19).

The new creation became the very goal and basic hope of the New Testament:

> This is a new creation. The old creation has gone [2 Cor. 5:16].

A new heaven and a new earth . . . I am making the whole
of creation new [Rev. 21:1, 5].
This was to create one single New Man . . . [Eph. 2:15].

Jesus himself is quoted as referring to the time "when all is
made new"(Mt. 19:28).

Science is convinced that a definitive and qualitative change
has taken place at the present time in the continuing creation
process, because its future direction is now in the hands of humankind itself, for the first time. As the result of a stunning
breakthrough, human beings now possess the knowledge of the
genetic code governing all life, and they have unlocked the very
secrets of matter and the forces of the universe. This leads us
to a startling new understanding of the biblical responsibility of
humankind to enter into the process of creation, to participate
in it, and to help God complete it: "Fill the earth and conquer
it. . . . Be masters of all living things" (Gen. 1:28).

The miracles of Jesus as recorded in the Gospels come
across in a new light, as examples of Jesus' participating in
continuing creation and being part of the earth process itself.
The word "miracle" is not used in the four Gospels to describe the actions of Jesus. "Miracle" is neither a biblical nor
a Jewish word. The Jewish Bible saw the same creative power
of God at work in the most ordinary actions of life as much
as in the extraordinary ones. God was creating when one over-
came a personal difficulty in life and when the Jewish armies
defeated an enemy. God was creating in the first meeting of
any young man with any young girl, in the stamping of feet
to frighten enemies, or in the violent blowing of wind across
the sea in the exodus.[13]

That wind, or Spirit, of God continued to blow through the
Old and New Testaments. It is not only the human being that
has Spirit. There has been Spirit hovering over all the world
since the beginning of creation. There is a spiritual meaning to
the world, to bread and wine and water, to humankind's envi-
ronment, and to the universe. The preeminence of Christ extends beyond humankind to all the things of the world. Jesus
showed this by using bread and wine and fish, and wind and

waves and water, and a paste made of clay in bringing healing and salvation to our world.

The word used in the New Testament for these actions of Jesus is not "miracle" but "sign," and that is different. That is sacrament: a sign pointing to the presence of the divine and the sacred in the world; a sign pointing to Jesus completely at ease in the midst of creation, handling material things, at home on the earth.

The "nature miracles" of Jesus are sometimes dismissed as being unworthy of belief. If they are looked at as special-effects tricks or super wonderworks, perhaps they are unbelievable. But if they are seen as portraying a person, Jesus, completely in consonance with the world of things and the earth from which he came; if they are seen as a sign of the presence of the creating, saving God whose domain extends beyond the souls of men and women to their bodies and to the whole world of creatures in which they are immersed; if they are viewed as extending to that "creation groaning and travailing even until now," as Paul describes it, "waiting for the revelation of the children of God" — then the actions of Jesus flow naturally and without violence to our faith.

"The promise of inheriting the world was made to Abraham and his descendants" (Rom. 4:13), and Jesus, this son of Abraham, was quietly living out that promise as he turned the water into wine, calmed the storm at sea, and walked across the angry waters. Creation was continuing as he directed his fishermen followers to a great catch, fed the multitudes in the desert with a few loaves of bread and some fish, and with the greatest reverence for good in an often starving world, gathered up what was left "so nothing would go to waste."

The writers of the Gospels make no distinction between ordinary and extraordinary actions of Jesus as they describe the godly kingdom of the waters of the Jordan and of the containers at Cana and of the pool of Siloam; the kingdom of the bread for people in the wilderness and the bread of the Last Supper; the kingdom of vineyard and grapes and wine of Cana and of the cup of the New Covenant; the kingdom of fish filling nets to breaking point at his command, and of fish for breakfast cooked by him in resurrection time. Jesus was depicted as the first true earthling on an earth becoming new.

The sacredness of the earth, the sacramental vision of the earth, is mediated to us through Jesus of Nazareth. Together with scientists we ponder that sacredness. Everything we know as human came from the earth. It was in the earth first. In the continuing process of creation, it could have come from no other place. The simplest and most complex forms of all living things came out of the earth — out of that inert, "lifeless" earth. Conscious life, intelligent life, spiritual life, faith life, Christian life, our very idea of God — they all came from the earth. They were in the earth first. It is not only our source of life. It is our primary source of revelation. The earth is much more sacred than we have supposed, much holier than we have treated it. It is not merely a storage closet from which we plunder resources, nor is it a garbage dump.[14]

Even the most sacred reality of our faith life and Christian life, our Savior and Redeemer, came out of the earth. He did not come riding to us from outer space on the chariot of the gods. He came from *here*. He is an earthling.

The old Advent hymn *Rorate Coeli* reminds us beautifully of this basic tenet of Christianity. After praying for the dew to drop down and the clouds to rain down *from heaven*, it concludes:

> Aperiatur terra, et germinet Salvatorem.
> (Let the earth open up, and bud forth a Savior.)

We people of the church need to be aware of what we believe as we join with others of this generation in the sacred task of "building the earth."

9

Preaching the Gospel to America

We have considered the crisis of our age and the convulsive shock waves it has sent across our world and our church. We have examined the characteristics of the age that is dying and the barely discernible features of the age that is being born. We have realized the vulnerability of a church that makes an absolute out of the age in which it has lived and refuses to move into the age that is dawning for humankind. We have looked at the necessity of refounding the church of Christ for our age, as much a matter of life and death for us as ever it was for the Judeo-Christian church of the first century. We have seen the stunted growth of *the Christ* and the deteriorating ministry and sacramental activity of the Western church. We have tried to find the proper sense and meaning of the presence of the church in the arena of the world and in the midst of creation.

Aware of, and taught by, all these realities, we finally come to the end of reflection and must face the very real problem that is pressing in on us—the preaching of the gospel to an actual people today, such as the American people. We are confronted with the formidable task of the evangelization of America.[1]

Evangelization is not the same thing as convert-making. Evangelization is essentially related to a culture, to a community. Convert-making is geared to individuals. Its success is based on numbers. The "conversion" referred to is a one-way street, pre-

124

determined and predictable. Evangelization is not the process of preaching to a vast gathering of people urging them to make a decision for Christ, according to the norms of the preacher who, along with his helpers, has already made that decision and is safely converted. It would be impossible to *convert* 240 million individual Americans. It is not only possible, it is essential to *evangelize* the American culture, or the many cultures that make up the American people. Evangelization means bringing the full force of the gospel to the American culture and letting the chips fall where they may, or where the Spirit lets them fall. Evangelization is essentially unpredictable. The outcome cannot be known ahead of time. The conversion, or *metanoia*, involved is a conversion of both the evangelist and the evangelized.

The gospel of the evangelization process is that message referred to many times in these pages—"the final and fundamental substance of the Christian message." It can be no other. With all cultural accretions peeled away from it, it is the heart of that message to which we must be faithful as we go about the task of refounding the church of Christ for this age. Being faithful to that message, which reflects the mind of Christ, we face the culture before us.

We open up dialogue with the American people, presenting this message to them as honestly and authentically as we can, allowing them the absolute right to reject it or to accept it. If they accept it, they must be free to understand it and to express it from the midst of their culture. One has to wonder if Americans have ever before been presented with that opportunity—white Americans or black Americans or Native Americans. And we, the evangelizers, must be sensitive enough to hear what they play back to us, to see if it does not give to us an even clearer vision and more refined view of that "naked gospel."

We must speak the language of the people. Language includes more than just words. It has to contain the richness, power, and emotions these words convey. We have to understand the mentality of the people being evangelized, their fears, their dreams, their history. Language will be the contact between us and the people being evangelized, and the gospel will pass from us to them along the path of that language. It may well affect that language. Many languages have been affected by the gospel. In history, languages have been evangelized by the gospel message, and the message itself has come alive and been enriched through those languages.

Culture is such a part of us that it is difficult to stand back and look at it for what it is. We are so at one with it that we are reluctant to think that it stands in need of evangelization and conversion. It is like being in the same room for a long time with a group of people. Perhaps there are good odors and aromas in the room like those of food or perfume or flowers, and bad odors like those of tobacco smoke or alcohol or worse, but our sense of smell becomes inured to the good and bad odors. Yet, if we get a chance to go out for a while into the bright sunshine or the night air, and then return to the room, the good and the bad odors assail the nostrils. We have to be like strangers, missionaries perhaps, who have never been in the room space of America, or have been away from it for a long time and are allowed to return to it. Then the odors and aromas, both good and bad, are strong and unmistakable. At that point we can begin to look on America with the restless eyes of a missionary.

Every culture has its high peaks of insights, ideals, and values reaching up and out, worthy of dialogue and transculturation and fulfillment by the gospel. Every culture also has its dark valleys of less noble traits and tendencies, waiting to be critiqued by that dialogue with, and opening to, other cultures, waiting to be covered over by the gospel. If Christ comes to a culture in the process of evangelization, something will live and something will die. Christ comes to fulfill every culture and to prophesy against every culture.

The American culture, or group of subcultures making up the society of America, is no exception. The very challenging task facing an evangelist in the process of dialogue in America is to be able to single out those peaks worthy of gospel fulfillment, and to have the courage to prophesy against those dark valleys that blot the landscape of America.

Those peaks and valleys are the apertures, the openings, the points of entry for the gospel, the contact for the dialogue of evangelization. They can be, at the same time, the obstacles to the gospel and the very opportunities that make the preaching of the gospel possible in the high-risk venture of evangelization. Millions of people clinging to a cultural blindness can create an inertia that makes widescale convert-making impossible. But that same inertia can be transformed by communal reflection into a dynamic force that motivates the process of evangelization and enables it to live.

The "final and fundamental substance of the Christian message," that stripped-down skeletal core of the gospel, will not remain long. Immediately, as the dialogue opens, it begins to take on the flesh and blood of the culture being evangelized. It is this fleshing out of the message that makes dialogue compelling and revelatory. The message itself will take on different emphases and flavors for different cultures. It will *sound* different. The preaching of the gospel to the United States will have an unmistakable American accent.

What would it sound like — the gospel to America?

A GIANT LEAP FOR HUMANKIND

Neil Armstrong steps down from the ladder of the spacecraft to make the first human footprint on the moon. What is happening? Are we too close to the event to be aware of its significance?

> I look up at your heavens made by your fingers,
> at the moon and stars you set in place —
> ah, what is man that you should spare a thought for him,
> the son of man that you should care for him?
> Yet you have made him little less than a god,
> You have crowned him with joy and splendor,
> made him lord over the work of your hands,
> set all things under his feet [Ps. 8:3–6].

Joining with the work of the creator, participating in creation, takes on a new and qualitatively different meaning for the people of this generation, for those who travel in space, who have opened the primal force of the universe and have unraveled the secret code of every living thing — a meaning that previous generations, including those who wrote the Bible, could not comprehend. Even the evolutionary process, the knowledge of which was a kind of revelation in itself, is essentially changed. Future evolutionary development is now in the hands of humankind itself, which is where God always meant it to be.

The words of Scripture take on a significance that could not be understood before: "Increase and multiply and fill the earth and conquer it. Be masters of all living things" (Gen. 1:28). That is the biblical definition of the human race. The word "Adam," in the plural, means "to have dominion over the earth." That is the only way to describe *Adam* — in the plural, as the human race essentially related to the earth, the earth finally becoming conscious, the "ecstasy" of the earth.[2] The gospel begins here in that creation and in this earth; it is the Good News spoken of by Isaiah, Paul, and Jesus. If there is a naked gospel, a "final and fundamental substance of the Christian message," this is part of it.

This gospel of creation is a corrective for a sectarian view of God, of truth, and of faith, and for an "otherworldly spirituality." Everyone on planet earth, every group or nation or culture, has a common origin and a common destiny. A gospel that is not as wide as the earth, that is without meaning for the whole earth, is no gospel at all. An ecumenism that does not include the earth and all the peoples of the earth is an empty word. The gospel begins with God the creator and God's creation. Everything else must flow out of this creation. We know God only in relation to creation and to humankind. We know God no other way. If there is a God beyond creation, we know nothing of such a God. The God of revelation is a God who stepped into human history, into earth history.

Creation is a biblical notion that must be learned. It is not grasped automatically or intuitively. It is not known outside the Bible except by those who have borrowed it from the Bible. It is not easily accepted by Americans, who are accustomed to thinking that the meaning of all objects is fully explained when the objects are measured, their laws described, their weights listed, and their numbers counted. People must learn, if they are to accept the gospel, that an object or a thing does not exist if God is not creating it at this moment; that God exists in creation, in every object, and that it is not idolatry or superstition

to believe so. That is the deepest meaning of anything in existence, and the reason science finds mystery just beyond everything it discovers.

A biblical writer asks a rhetorical query:

Who carves a channel for the downpour,
and hacks a way for the rolling thunder,
so that rains may fall on lands where no one lives,
and the deserts devoid of human dwelling,
giving drink to the lonely wastes
and making grass spring where everything was dry?
[Job 38:25–27]

In response to the question the writer depicts a very active
and concerned creator behind even the plant that blooms in the
desert and "wastes its beauty on the desert air." From inanimate
to animate to animal instinct, a divine author is posited:

Do you find a prey for the lioness
and satisfy the hunger of her whelps? . . .
Does the hawk take flight on your advice
when he spreads his wings to travel South?
[Job 38:39; 39:26]

We must come, at last, to understand that our primary revelation is creation, the unwritten book, as sacred as any published one. The ancient Babylonians knew this when they
referred to the stars as "the silent writings of the heavens." The
Psalmist agrees:

The heavens declare the glory of God,
the vault of heaven proclaims his handiwork;
day discourses of it to day,
night to night hands on the knowledge,
No utterance at all, no speech,
no sound that anyone can hear;
yet their voice goes out through all the earth,
and their message to the ends of the world [Ps. 19:1–4].

Those last two verses are used in the liturgy of the Feast of St. Peter and St. Paul to describe the apostles, those first preachers of the gospel. And no wonder. It is the very same gospel being described in both places.

The revelation goes on, from the heavens, from the written Scriptures—sharp brilliant pictures like the pictures the astronauts gave us on their way to the moon, shining pictures of the loveliest planet in the solar system, the blue-white planet against the black background of space. Our salvation is identified with that planet.

"To Yahweh belongs the earth, and all who live in it" (Ps. 24:1). Our Christianity arises out of that earth and out of creation. Our sacraments come from the earth, from water of the blue planet, from oil made from plants and fruits, from bread of grain and wine of grapes (fruit of the earth, fruit of the vine), from human hands joined and words of vows spoken. Our spirituality comes from the earth, our holiness. It is not meant to be a spirituality or a holiness apart from the earth, in flight from the earth. Americans have never had a spirituality of their own. Their spirituality has never been taken seriously by Europeans or by people of the third world. They are accused of being worldly and materialistic. They must develop a spirituality of the world, a *spirituality of the earth*.[3]

Authentic Christian prayer has its roots in creation, in people opening themselves to the creative power of God, allowing the power of creation to continue to work in them to make all things possible, participating themselves in that work of creation and in the answer to their own prayers.

Young Americans in increasing numbers are finding it difficult to take part in a "Christian religion" that is becoming ever more artificial, irrelevant to their real human lives. The deeper the crisis grows in our age and in their young experience, the more artificial and narrow and hypocritical and sanctuary-bound and unexciting we become. Meanwhile, the membership in our parish churches, even the "big" ones, grows older and older, and funerals are beginning to become the main feature of our ministry. We must honestly search to find if Christ has meaning, after all, for young people of our age, the Christ who came "that they might have life, and live it to the full." If we cannot find that meaning, then we have no hope for young people in our church.

There are other pictures that come to mind in regard to the earth—dark, disturbing, terrible pictures: Hiroshima, Nagasaki, Three Mile Island, Bhopal, Chernobyl, Love Canal, the James River, criminal disposal of toxic waste, towns being evacuated because of chemical spills. And in fiction, the chilling picture of the head of the Statue of Liberty, with one spike protruding upward from her crown, lying in the wasteland sand of New York Island, in the final scene of *Planet of the Apes*.

Americans have not always lived up to their splendid gifts and endowments and calling. They have plundered the sacred earth in the name of commerce, despoiling it of treasures that can never be replaced, using up resources not in proportion to their population relative to the world's population but in proportion to their wealth and acquired needs. In an hour of anguish and doubt, they became the only nation in history to unleash atomic destruction against another nation. Today they stand as one of just two nations on earth that could reduce all higher life on this planet to thermonuclear oblivion. And slowly they allow air, earth, and water to become receptacles of garbage that is poisonous, meanwhile looking up to the sky for another planet on which to begin all over again. Americans as a people have sinned, and Americans as a people need conversion.

Jesus of Nazareth knew what was meant by a broken world, a broken humanity, a broken heart—all in need of healing. He took them all into his hands, along with the bread, and offered them up, saying, "This is my body, broken for you."

THE UNPREACHED GOSPEL

There is a game that can be played with American school children, whether of high school or intermediate school age, and the outcome of the game can be fairly accurately predicted ahead of time. Ask them if they are really free, as Americans so earnestly dream of being free, and tell them that you are going to test them to see how free they are. Ask them to name one appliance of American technology which they are now using, without which they could live in contentment.

Could you do without a refrigerator? They answer, "Of course not, food would go bad, and soft drinks don't taste any good hot."

Without a car in your family? "No, shopping centers are so far away."

A stereo? "No." *Air conditioning? A television? Color television? Cable vision? M.T.V.? Designer Jeans?* "No" to all of them.

A telephone? The answer "No!" is deafening and unanimous.

There is no use going any further. No matter how far you progress, you find that most American children cannot "live" today without appliances to which they have become accustomed, even if some of those items were not in existence five or ten years ago. And five or ten years from now, they will not be able to live without gadgets that do not yet exist today.

American children are not free. They are the targets of some of the most massive mind conditioning ever let loose on human beings, and their parents are willing accomplices in this process. As a result, we have produced a generation of young people almost immune to the gospel. How can the Sermon on the Mount or the teachings of Jesus about the dangers of riches and possessions ever reach children who are indoctrinated with the ideals of status and money and who have become fierce defenders of private property and converts to the belief that happiness is synonymous with a multitude of possessions? It can be questioned whether American children are ever presented with the gospel teachings in any serious manner, or whether they would, today, be capable of understanding them even if they were. There is too much around them in American society and in their parents' lives that gives the lie to the gospel. We must remember that we are talking about evangelization, not convert-making. There are individual exceptions to this attitude, but here we are not focusing on individuals, rather on cultures, which are the arenas of evangelization. It is undeniably true that Americans, as a people, stand in need of a change of heart, of conversion.

It is altogether fitting that the Gospels use a young man as the example of a person so blinded by possessions that he passes up the opportunity to follow Jesus and walk permanently in his company. Young people should be presented with this story in all its starkness, although it would probably be unfair to ask them which one appliance of modern technology they would be willing to sacrifice in order to follow Christ.

It is not fair to focus on young people in America, because it is not certain that their parents accept any more easily the demands of the gospel. Indeed, this part of the gospel has never truly been preached in America, despite the fact that this particular message takes up one-tenth of all the verses of the Synoptic Gospels, and an even greater proportion of the Gospel of Luke considered by itself. This conspiracy of silence, hardly an accident, is an astonishing fact of American church life. It is easier to talk about love in American churches than about the risk of money and possessions, even though Jesus spoke much more about the latter. It is next to impossible to convey a trust in divine providence in the face of the barrage of messages about security and investments and savings and I.R.A.s.

It is heresy to suggest that education can possibly have any other purpose than the acquiring of a good job, or that compassion and concern for others have any place in the consuming drive for success. Advertisements for everything from beer to clothes to cars to airlines appeal to the crassest instincts of young and upwardly mobile men and women. Finally, it is useless to preach the words of Jesus that "one cannot serve God and money" when the churches of God continue to use money as the primary criterion for parochial, ministerial, and Christian well-being.

All this sounds like a bleak appraisal of Christian society in the United States, but, as evangelists, we cannot turn off our restless missionary eyes. We can evangelize a people only as they are, not as we would like them to be. Any missionary, looking at the American scene, would see only a bad missionary situation. In the eyes of any missionary, the greatest single obstacle in America to the gospel and to the practice of Christianity is surely Americans' attitude toward possessions and their singular worship of money and what it can procure.

We need reflection on the graphic story told by Luke about the rich man (called Dives in the Latin Vulgate) and the poor man named Lazarus. The story is striking in implying that Dives, in the best-case scenario, is running a terrible risk simply by possessing great riches. In the worst-case scenario, the riches constitute an absolute obstacle to God for Dives, creating a situation in which he will never again be able to experience God, in this life or the next. The story becomes more exasperating. Jesus links Dives and Lazarus so closely in the story that he implies Lazarus is poor and suffering *because* Dives is rich and well filled, and vice versa. Jesus further shows in his parable that God is not impartial between the two of them. God is very partial, and stands squarely on the side of the poor man.

Dives and Lazarus can stand for many things in our world, for individuals or entire peoples. Lazarus is the person on welfare, willing to eat the scraps that fall from our table, with food stamps and surplus cheese and butter. Lazarus is street people and the starving and sick peoples of the world. Dives stands for individuals—and for us Americans. Who else, as a people, so clearly fits the description? We do eat well, even magnificently; we are enslaved to changing fashions—dressing in purple and fine linens; we live comfortably, using up the resources of the world. At our gate (probably locked) just outside our property, lies Lazarus—hungry, ill clothed, unappealing, frightening, even disgusting. Like Dives, we do not seem to realize the danger in our possessions, nor to be aware of the gulf between us and God because of them. We do not seem to recognize that, in this matter, God is not on our side. Claiming Moses and the prophets and the Bible as our own and having someone rise from the dead are no guarantee that we shall be convinced otherwise.

WHAT DO YOU BELIEVE?

If you make an effort to search honestly for the gospel, the search can yield many surprises and advantages. One of the advantages is the discovery that the basic message of Christianity is manageable, knowable. Every Muslim can explain the basic tenets of his or her belief. So each Muslim becomes a teacher of Islam. The average American Catholic would be embarrassed and hard pressed to give an adequate explanation of Christianity in public, for instance in church. You should be able to address a parish community and ask, "What do you believe? Those of you who go to church regularly, spend so much time in church and in church activities — it is necessary to render an account of your belief, to give meaning and substance to your lives. It is important for the meaning of church, for the meaning of your activities, your worship — important liturgically to ask, 'What do you believe?' "

It makes a great difference if you believe in a God who loves only good people, prosperous people, industrious people, and loves them only at such times as they are all of these things; or in the God who loves also evil people, "worthless" people, lazy people, people on welfare and a drain on society; a God who loves us all no matter how good or how evil we are.

Do we believe in a God who judges all people as we do, and finds some who are unworthy of forgiveness? Do we spend our time in church thanking God we are not like the rest of people, condemning those not like ourselves, and imagining it is a Christian thing to do so? Do we go to church on a Sunday morning with our minds completely made up, determined that what we think and feel and believe as we enter that church will not be changed at all; that we will leave it exactly as we enter it and that nothing that is said or done in that worship will change our minds, our convictions, our prejudices, our faith, as we go about our role as participant, usher, communicant, reader, or minister — locked into ourselves in a deadly blindness and deafness that is impervious to the command of Christ and of our baptism: *Ephphetha*, Be thou opened?

Sometimes we need a jolt in the preaching of the gospel that opens up to us the part of the gospel that has been hidden from us. Such a jolting revelation can come in different ways, sometimes in the most surprising and unexpected manner. One version of *Godspell* was like that. In that presentation, the friendly clownlike character portraying Jesus told a story: "Two men went to the temple to pray. One stood there confidently looking up to heaven, listing his accomplishments," quite determined to leave the temple exactly as he had entered it — unchanged — "thanking God he was not like the rest of men, especially that other member of the congregation kneeling there." Everybody in the temple knew what a sinner he was.

The clown portraying the first man in the story walked forward as Jesus was talking, preening himself, completely pleased with himself, hugging himself in pure narcissistic pleasure. Jesus continued: "The other man went to the temple, feeling completely unworthy to be there, not even daring to look up to heaven, and asked for mercy on himself, a sinner." The clown who acted out this person's part stayed in the rear, knelt down awkwardly, and made a gesture with two fingers and a facial expression that immediately identified him as the most detested and disgraced public servant and president America ever had. The audience laughed. Then "Jesus," pointing to the pitifully kneeling figure, said the startling words: "But I say to you, this man went home from the temple justified," and then pointing to the preening popinjay, "Not this one. . . ."

The scene was like a slap in the face or a blow to the stomach for everyone in the audience. Until the moment at which the members of the audience recognized the kneeling man, they had automatically identified themselves with the "hero" of the story—that kneeling "publican." Suddenly, that was impossible—to identify with that hated figure on the stage—and the truth and power of the parable came home. In truth, we, in our lives and in our churches, have always been that other figure, the haughty, self-satisfied one, the one who thanked God he was not like the rest of the people. Sometimes it takes a realistic modern setting to understand the gospel message.

We consistently read the Gospel stories backwards, placing ourselves in the role of the heroes and heroines, and thus miss the thrust of the story. We become the humble publican, the prodigal, become the humble son, or the forgiving father, not the resentful elder brother who does not believe in forgiveness, which is who we are really meant to be in the story. We fancy ourselves as Lazarus the poor man, or the workers hired at the eleventh hour in the vineyard, or the guests from East and West welcomed to the wedding banquet. And especially we see ourselves as the Good Samaritan. That is hardly the purpose of the parables and stories of the Gospels. The theme of the gospel is not "I'm O.K., you're O.K.," although it is often mistaken for that distorted message.

INDIVIDUALISM, SELF-FULFILLMENT, AND RACISM

Once, Jacob had made a soup, and Esau returned from the countryside exhausted. Esau said to Jacob, "Let me eat that red soup there; I am exhausted. . . . " Jacob said, "First, sell me your birthright, then." Esau said, "Here I am at death's door; what use will my birthright be to me?" Then Jacob said, "First, give me your oath"; he gave him his oath and sold his birthright to Jacob . . . and after eating and drinking he got up and went. That was all Esau cared for his birthright [Gen. 25:29–34].

The preaching of the gospel in the American accent must come face to face with the fact that the creed of stark and rugged individualism running through the fiber of our society, through our business and economic and spiritual world, has nothing to do with Christianity. We should not baptize it. We should exorcise it from our midst. What meaning can Christianity possibly have outside all community, in the arena of destructive individualism?

Individualism is not the same as personalism. *Individualism* is an exclusivity, a refusal of mutual sharing or interpenetration or dependence. *Personalism* is an essential interrelatedness toward growth and meaning. All persons have immense possibilities for what they can become and accomplish. There is an almost infinite value and worth to a person. Americans understand this and believe it. In this sense, they are the true successors of the fathers of the church of the fourth century, who first opened the way to the modern notion of person in their reflections on the Trinity, transforming the idea of *persona* — the mask behind which ancient actors hid their real personalities. Open to the whole world of people and things, a person is capable of any development and growth, and is not limited by birth or blood or upbringing.

But the other side of the coin is individualism, lonely, destructive individualism, which depends and relies on no one else and shares neither concern nor responsibility for anyone else — as though every person were truly an island. In the life of faith it affects one's attitude toward faith and prayer and holiness and salvation. It distorts the Christian message. Perhaps to the ancient controversy—whether it is by faith or by good works that a person is saved—we must add the modern question: "Whether by faith or by good works, can any persons be saved by themselves?"

The story of Jacob and Esau needs retelling for us. We Catholics are not Jacob, crafty and chosen. We are Esau, slow and vulnerable and somewhat despised.

Once America was a land of bounty and promise. And the Catholic church, in its poor, came here dispirited and hungry for the good life. All the church had was its birthright of centuries—a sacred commitment to community, a faith shared in a body, a sense of corporate identity. "Give me some of the good life," it asked. But America said, "first, sell me your birthright, your foreignness, your idea of a worldwide brotherhood, your belief in Christianity as community. It does not belong here." The church said, "Here I am weak and powerless. What good will my birthright do me?" The church sold its birthright to America, so that it might belong and thrive in the land of plenty. The church sold its birthright for a bowl of soup, for a mess of pottage. That was all it cared for its birthright.

Those with ears to hear, let them hear.

It is a strange phenomenon to have America, a country so puritanical in its background and origins, leading the world in the flood of sexual exploitation and obsession. Pornography and sexual abandon in films, television programs, music, and advertising; crusades for birth control and abortion—all are part of the lifestyle to which the upwardly mobile generation, all those born after World War II, the "baby-boomer" generation, has become accustomed. Margaret Mead once described this segment of the population as the other end of the generation gap. Self-gratification is as old as the human race, but using that demand for self-gratification as the criterion for all one's actions is disturbingly new in our society. Popular psychologists and even teachers of ethics and religion have responded to that demand, and have created for us a "middle-class morality" that is staggering in its implications. The deeper sin in all these pleasurable pursuits is not a sexual sin, but the sin of selfishness on a scale unknown before.

We should face the fact that, as a people, we have rejected the words of Jesus: "If anyone wants to be a follower of mine, he must deny his very self, take up his cross and follow me." To deny oneself is utterly un-American—counter to the overriding demands for self-gratification, self-fulfillment, self-salvation. It might be better if we stopped playing around with the gospel of Jesus Christ. It might be better if we simply rejected it—better for us and for the gospel.

The American bishops' pastoral letter on racism, "Brothers and Sisters to Us," may be the best-kept secret of the Catholic church in America today. But it is no secret that racism in America and in the American church is the *original* sin. From the earliest days of the church in America until the most recent outbursts of black anger and humiliation, the American church has been riddled with racism, from top to bottom, from diocesan structure to religious life.

Racism has been compared to a terrible disease. Like a disease, it is infectious and highly contagious. It is passed on from parents to children. It has infected every institution. There are many carriers of the disease, some of them unknowing and unconscious carriers. Virulent outbreaks occur from time to time. One has to ask the unavoidable question: "If racism is a disease in America—is it an incurable disease?" We have to admit honestly that we do not know the answer to that question.

One thing is certain, as far as religion is concerned: the Catholic church owes an apology to the American black. And that apology, that request for forgiveness, must be made on the scale of the pope's first visit, since the time of St. Peter, to a Jewish synagogue—Pope John Paul II's historic journey to the synagogue of Rome. We Americans must try to answer in a real way that haunting question of the Gospel: "Who is my neighbor?"

When Jesus first told the story of the Samaritan galloping down the high road to Jericho, his listeners must have been shocked to hear who the hero of the story turned out to be. They assuredly did not like it and were undoubtedly stunned by the outcome and the question: "Who was neighbor to the one who fell among thieves?" It was a kind of transcultural shock.

A missionary today, preaching the gospel to good peoples who have never heard it, does not have time or need to explain the history of the animosity of Jewish and Samaritan peoples that gives meaning to the original story. The missionary must find a way to express the meaning of this important story—not its historical accidentals—so as to keep alive the shocking power of the story. A missionary to the pastoral cattle herders of East Africa, for example, might convey the full force of the story by making the hero of the story, not one of their own pastoral people, but a hated outsider, a barbaric farmer. And thus the story of the good and merciful farmer carries the same message to a pastoral people as the Samaritan story did to the Jews. Both the Jews and the East African pastoralists feel as if they have been assaulted with a blow to the stomach or a slap across the face with such a story.

What would the story of the Good Samaritan sound like with an American accent? I am afraid there is not that much difference between an African non-Christian audience and a modern American one—especially a young audience—when it comes to knowing the difference between Samaritan and Jew. How, then, would you have to tell the story to get across the same idea that Jesus did with his famous parable? With the same salvific force? I think it could go something like this:

Once upon a time, not long ago, a young girl was making her way home from work very late at night. She had almost reached home when, suddenly, a crazed and wild man jumped out of the bushes with a big knife and began attacking the girl. He stabbed her. She fought back and screamed for help. Twice she broke away from him and ran, but he caught up with her. She continued to struggle to get away and to cry aloud for help. The struggle continued for half an hour. Her screams for help were heard in all the nearby apartment buildings. Some people actually looked out the window and saw her fighting for her life.

One man was tempted to go down to her aid, but was sorely afraid for his life and did not go. Another women heard her cry, saw her struggling, and was going to call the police, but was reluctant to get involved in the official questioning that would surely follow. It would be nice to be able to say that someone finally went to help her and saved her life — but that is not true. The truth is that thirty-six people heard or saw Kitty Genovese screaming for help that night in New York City, and not one came to her aid by so much as a phone call to the police. No one. And she was killed after a half-hour of struggle and terror.

Do you want to hear the story of the Good Samaritan as it must be preached to America? It is the story of Kitty Genovese. In the story of the Samaritan as told with an American accent, the answer to the question "Who is my neighbor?" is: *There is no Good Samaritan*. No one wants to get involved.

Those who have ears to hear, let them hear.

A NEW AGE DAWNING

In chapter 2 I spoke of Sorokin's description of the new age that is upon us as an Ideational age in which a unified spiritual system of thought and action, based on a single principle, will dominate the world of tomorrow. Whether the age will be called the age of the Global Village, or the Information age, or the Postindustrial age, or the age of the World Church, or the Ecological age, that single dominating idea will emerge. We saw that the search for that unifying principle might be the most important quest of our lifetime. The form that idea will take can be ascertained at this time in only the vaguest, most germinal outline.

It will almost certainly have to do with the earth, the entire earth. The time has come to dream of a new earth, said Teilhard de Chardin. The crisis of our time is not just a crisis of the Western world or of modern humankind, but a crisis of the earth in its most complete dimensions. Humankind, of course, will always be the most important factor of every time, but in this dawning age of a "creative tomorrow" (Sorokin), we shall turn from a consideration of humankind in exclusion to a consideration of the earth as a whole, with humankind realizing its responsibility for the entire human process and earth process, and the earth, through humankind, finally becoming conscious of itself on a global scale. This age will come to realize that there is a world to be built — not a nation, not a continent, but a world. As startling as this might sound, such a thought will become the accepted, commonplace thing of the future. Once it is clear that this is the direction in which all life is moving, and that it is the only way of saving our world, we shall have to say "Yes!" to that direction.[4]

Every Ideational age has followed a Sensate age in which excessive, exclusive attention has been paid to the sensory and the physical — always to the detriment of the spiritual. The Sensate age — the individualistic, scientific, technological age — that has preceded our time is no exception. It has brought us degeneration and exhaustion, and we are near to annihilation and destruction.

This new age dawning upon us shows everywhere signs of a new awareness of the sacred all around us. The recovery of the sacred, which had been banished from our world, has tremendous psychic dynamism and implications. Everywhere, in every field of thought, we are perceiving that the psychic and the physical are complementary dimensions of each other. Something is happening to the whole structure of human consciousness. Some describe it, rather, as the "collective unconscious," using the words of Jung. Conscious or unconscious, it can also be seen as the continuing pouring out of the Spirit on all humankind.[5]

The word "sacred" now has a meaning much wider than before, an appreciation that revives the whole world of symbolism, no longer considered superstitious and darkness, a realization that it is through symbolism and the sacramental vision, and not by pure scientific analysis and description alone, that humankind establishes the most vital contact with the realities of life.

The single idea, the simple principle, the unified spiritual system of thought and action of the dawning age will have to do with the planet earth and nothing less, with humankind controlling the building of that earth.

To speak of evangelization in the midst of this cosmic approach seems narrow, provincial, irrelevant, outdated. Yet it is the relationship of evangelization to cultures and the religions they enshrine that makes it absolutely essential. No religion in the world, including Christianity, is adequate to the issues at stake today. No religion, no ethics, no cultural form, no social or political structure, no ideology can support the future that is upon us. We have always looked for light and guidance from the great religious traditions, yet mere internal extensions of existing religions will not be enough for today. Their interpenetration and mutual fecundation are now imperative. This convergence and growth through dialogue as all religions enter fully into the human process and earth process must be in a manner never before experienced. The dialogue that Christianity must enter into today is not an academic, clubby, luxurious endeavor. It is a matter of life and death for our world.[6]

Evangelization is essentially a dialogue, a free dialogue with the cultures of the world and the religious ideas they uphold. It will be no good if we Christians enter into this living dialogue without being open to conversion to a fuller truth. Neither will it be of any value if we water down the Christian message to make it more palatable to Hindus, Buddhists, Muslims, the peoples of traditional religion, and those of the scientific-technological culture, with whom we enter into dialogue. We must bring to them, in all honesty and humility, the full brunt of the Christian message, letting the chips fall where they may.

What is the message that we bring? It is a message of God who is a Spirit totally beyond us, yet is the creator of this world, a God who loves this world and is saving it; who loves good and evil people, forgives all who turn to God, is prodigal (generous in gifts and calling), continues to create to wipe out suffering and injustice, promises to save all men and women, all nations — the whole world. We are called to be perfect as God is perfect, forgiving all, reaching out to the suffering, in the sacred task of building the earth.

It is a message of Jesus Christ. God spoke one time. We hear that Word twice: the spontaneous *creation* of the word, and the *begetting* of God's only Son. In contrast to idols, human-made inferior images of God, God creates in divine image (first, a partial image, Adam, and then the perfect image, Jesus). It is a matter of continuing creation. Jesus participates in that continuing creation and in building the earth by bringing the kingdom, which is the world the way God meant it to be. Jesus incorporates the things of this world into his encounter with human beings, showing that his preeminence extends through all creation. We do not meet Christ by escaping from the earth. Jesus images God in all acts of creation as a lover and forgiver and healer. In his cross he passes on the obligation to all of his followers to deny their very selves in service to others. The resurrection is the beginning of the new creation. The second coming will complete it. The Holy Spirit, the Spirit of Christ, was there at the beginning of time as creation began, and will lead humankind to its completion. We must work for the world the way God meant it to be—until Christ comes.

When we further simplify the message, strip it to its naked, bare bones, it sounds something like this:

Short formula

God, the totally other, is the creator of our world, and as such is provident, loving, forgiving, just, generous, partial to the poor, to the suffering and the weak, and is the Savior of all. Humankind is the image of God, imperfect though it be, and is called to participate in the creative acts of God.

Jesus Christ is the Son of God, Emmanuel, God with us, and the created image of God as a true human, in whom the offer of salvation is made to us. Jesus is so perfectly human, so perfectly the image of God, that we must call him God appearing in the universe. As perfect image of the unseen God, Jesus participates in all the creative acts of God, and in bringing the kingdom, meant for this world but opening to the world beyond and to the absolute. Jesus brings human freedom of body and soul from any kind of servitude, liberation from anything that oppresses humankind. Jesus was crucified and died and rose from the dead to save us. Jesus promises and sends the Spirit. Jesus Christ will come again.

This is the message we must bring totally, unashamedly, yet humbly to the dialogue with the peoples and cultures of the world, as we search for a fuller truth. Burdened with all the shortcomings of the language in which it is expressed, it is naked—or, rather, fleshless—waiting for the incarnation that will come to it from the nations. It is not new or startling, but it is compelling to those who have never heard it or reflected on it. In a stammering, incomplete, awkwardly expressed way, it is the final and fundamental substance of the Christian message. This is the message that Isaiah and Jesus and Paul have passed to us, and which we in turn must pass on to a world caught between the last light of a dying yesterday and the bright morning of a creative tomorrow. This is the gospel that we preach.

10

Epilogue: The Response

THE CHURCH

The First Meeting

It began with a forlorn group of black parishioners and a white priest meeting in the church office. There were eleven blacks — seven women, four men — dispirited members of a dying parish, as so many black Catholic parishes are today. They were gathered for the first Bible study and reflection meeting. The priest sat at the desk and the people spread themselves around the office. They had agreed to meet and discuss the Gospel of St. Luke. The priest recited an opening prayer, and one after the other they started reading the first chapter aloud. There was an awkward silence at the conclusion of the reading, so the priest started explaining some of the technical background of the Gospel: who wrote it, the material he used as sources for his book, and what kinds of things to look for as the Gospel story unfolded.

Finally, a woman interrupted the monologue and said how surprised she was that in the Gospel story women spoke out so freely against the traditional way of doing things — in this case, the naming of a newborn son. The discussion switched to the Virgin Mary, and there were mixed feelings about her — teenage, unwed mother that she was. There was just too much experience in the room with teenage pregnancies, children having children, to leave the story of the Annunciation in a purely pious setting. The participants were also surprised at the radical, nonpious,

146

modern-sounding wording of Mary's prayer, the Magnificat: dragging down the mighty from their thrones and sending the rich away empty. It did not sound too holy.

After the discussion had gone on for some time, the woman who had first spoken suggested that, instead of going on to a new chapter the next time, they continue thinking about the first chapter. The priest had to agree, and if he had any plans for a systematic covering of the Gospel of Luke, he forgot about them.

The Second Meeting

The meeting moved to the parish house dining room, which was bigger than the office, because twenty people showed up for the second Bible reflection. The woman who had started the discussion in the first meeting sat at the head of the table, and the priest moved to the side. The woman opened with a prayer, which was slightly awkward, halting, and ungrammatical.

The discussion took off immediately. The example of Zechariah questioning God's messenger prompted someone to feel sympathy for him because in her own life she too had asked, "Why me, God?" Her young husband had died of cancer. She was devastated. The futility of death, the fear of death became the subject of discussion—the terror of long, lingering, drawn-out death. They had moved from the Bible to their own problems. Someone had witnessed the great service a hospice volunteer had provided to a dying person he knew. Shouldn't the church be involved in the same service to incurably ill patients as the hospice group provides? And handicapped people—what are Christians doing for them?

The Third Meeting

The numbers of the Bible study group grew to thirty and the meeting had to be held in the church hall. If more people should come, the group would have to divide. Someone volunteered to have the second group meet in his apartment in the nearby housing project. It was better that way, since the makeup of the parish, as was soon discovered, was not strictly homogeneous. Some people lived in the inner city. Others did not. And when they spoke of the same problems, they had different meanings. Crime, for example. Those who lived outside the inner city thought of crime in a refined, middle-class kind of way. Those of the inner city and the housing projects knew of crime in a more real, immediate way—terrifying in-the-streets, present-at-the-door crime.

One thing was certain, though. The people of God had been silent for centuries. Now it was time for them to speak. The discussion of the Holy Family of Nazareth took an unexpected turn. That family did not seem so flawless and tranquil and perfect after all. There was that threat of divorce hanging over the family from the beginning. There was grinding poverty—the offering of two pigeons in the Temple as the best the family of Nazareth could come up with, to redeem their first-born. There was the incident of the runaway child of twelve, with Jesus being scolded by his mother for his efforts, and the beginning of a generational conflict between mother and son, which continues through the Gospel. And it seems the family turned into a one-parent family, with Joseph disappearing from the scene. The Holy Family was becoming very familiar to the black group discussing it.

Further Meetings

The Bible study eventually broke up into three groups, two of them meeting in different neighborhoods, and one meeting at the church. Prayer became less awkward. The discussions became wide-ranging, and the priest could not attend all of the meetings.

Jesus became more human in the discussions and was seen as more identified with the lives and problems of the people present. He knew about muggings along the high road to Jericho. Like most of the blacks in the group he was only one or two steps removed from actual crime or criminals. He, too, had mixed with a bad crowd and was criticized for it. The despiritualized Beatitudes of Luke about the truly poor—the hungry, the weeping, the ones who are hated and abused and denounced as criminals—touched a sensitive nerve among the blacks discussing the Gospel story.

Those in the dismal housing projects saw some hope, and decided against despairing and giving up. They realized that, out of human respect and physical fear, they had been giving up their city and their neighborhood—block by block, street by street, house by house, floor by floor—to the criminal element in the city. They determined to take it back. There was going to be opposition, of course, from some tough youths who liked things the way they were and wanted no change.

BASIC COMMUNITY

Each group developed in its own way, but there were common characteristics. The reality of the community took on an importance that it never seemed to have had under parish auspices. The members grew very close to one another and shared many things that they had never shared before. They began to look on community as the essential element in the whole process. They seemed almost exclusive to outsiders, but they were really open to anyone who wanted to join them—even the priest. He found out that was exactly what he had to do. He had to ask to be accepted by them. They even gave the impression of being "anti-clerical," but they really were not. They were just more independent and responsible than anything he had experienced before in a church group. They began to look on the community not only as the heart of what they were doing, but as one of the sources of its correctness, of its inspiration, of its revelation. The other source was the Bible—the gospel.

The reflections on the gospel led to much more specific discussion of actual events and situations. And they moved away from personal problems to group problems. They talked openly of racism, of discrimination in the city and in the church. They began to make plans to combat these evils and became quite adept at planning and campaigning and politicking. They really did not care if the adversary was society or the hierarchical church.

Strangely enough (or maybe not so strangely), they became more prayerful. And they had a desire to ritualize their prayer. Perhaps it was the African blood in them. They made up ceremonies—*agapes*, with bread and grape juice. (They were wary

of alcohol and what it was doing to black society.) They celebrated different things — minor victories in their campaigns and
activities, and defeats and reversals as well. If the priest happened to be present, they asked him to complete the celebration
with the words of institution over the bread and wine (for those
who wanted to partake of the cup). The ensuing Eucharists were
strange to behold. They began with Bible study, serious and
prayerful, and filled with personal reflections, witnessing, and
confessions. They continued as very practical business meetings,
with plans of action, reports on continuing activities, and financial discussions. They ended with the breaking of the bread and
the blessing of the cup. They sang hymns as the Spirit moved
them.

They concentrated on young people, especially young black
males, even exerting social pressure on them at times. They
ritualized that process, too, into a kind of rite of passage. The
parents, and other elders of skill and wisdom, were called in to
pass on their wisdom in an effort to overcome the destructive
influence that American society was having on young black
males. They were addressed very plainly and unmistakably about
sex, drugs, and crime. And about health, too. Black males die
disproportionately younger than females from high blood pressure and heart problems. Their junk-food diet is abominable.
They have abandoned their African ancestors' respect for elders
and have taken on the uniquely American attitude of expecting
home life to be dominated by the whims and wishes of young
people and children. During the ceremony, the young person
was required to give an account of himself or herself including
expectations and goals in life. If a conversion was called for from
a way of life that was hurting the person and others, the young
person was asked to make a promise to that effect. At that point,
the priest was asked to be present to give a sign of forgiveness
to the young person in the name of the community, and to anoint
the person with strength for life's tasks. No confession was necessary. Everyone knew the young person's sins.

When a baby was born, they had a celebration that looked
like a baby shower because of the presents given, but it was
really a naming ceremony in which a grandparent held the baby
at arms' length, high in the air, offering it to God, after an-

nouncing its name publicly and whispering in the baby's ear a secret name that only the grandparent knew. Both the public name by which the baby would henceforth be known, and the secret name, were chosen very carefully, not so much for their sound as for their meaning. The parents and others spoke of the beauty and holiness of the child and of the unknown, limitless possibilities that lay before the child—possibilities known only to God. The whole community had the responsibility of allowing those possibilities to unfold. To celebrate the beauty of the moment, the child was baptized with the name it had just received, in the Name of the Trinity.

People who were not Catholics joined the group without becoming Catholics. Their baptisms were recognized as sufficient for membership. The community, in its outreach, did not set up Catholic organizations where other organizations, Protestant or secular, existed. They did not compete with these other organizations. They joined forces with them and became involved in things they had not considered before: homes for runaway children like the young Jesus; food for the elderly and the hungry. Before the Eucharist on every major feast day or holiday, they invited people in from the street, strangers, to take part in the ceremony. These street people listened to the Bible discussion, the work discussion, ate the meal prepared just for them, and took part in the Eucharist if they so wished. The group worked with those dealing with victims of crimes and with criminals in the jails.

There was tremendous change in their attitudes toward the church and its ministers. But perhaps the greatest change was in themselves and in their view of Christ. Christ—whom they recognized in that runaway boy, Jesus, in that one who came from a troubled family, who died a criminal's death—for this community became a black Christ. It did not happen overnight, but, as they considered their own position more and more, the position of the oppressed and persecuted people, they saw that the God who stands on the side of the oppressed would stand on the side of the blacks. And so would Christ, who would be identified with blacks. Christ would become black.

This simple realization and conviction is like a prism, which captures all the light and breaks it down into its component

rays; or like a laser beam that directs the light with pure inten-
sity. Everything else seems to flow from this dynamic insight.
And just as the Greeks were justified in seeing the Christ as the
Christus Victor, Pantocrator, and Sun God; and as the Middle
Ages saw in Christ the Ransomer, the One who makes satisfaction; and as Luther saw in Christ the One who achieves reconciliation with God in a free and sovereign act—so, today, blacks
have a right to see Christ as the black Christ, the Christ of the
oppressed, the Christ who is the blessedness of the Beatitudes,
the Christ identified with the poor and hungry and persecuted
and accursed. This interpretation of Christ is related to reality
in the historical Jesus, to a real facet of his life, just as much as
realities and facets of his life gave rise to the images of Christ
of the fathers of the church, of Byzantium, of the Middle Ages,
of the age of the reformers. The black Christ focuses, with an
intense light, on the black situation today in America, in South
Africa, and on people of color throughout the world.

All the liturgies and sacraments participated in by people of
this "Bible community" were intimate, and intensely related to
the liturgy of the black reality—the death and life, the defeats
and victories of that reality. Their Eucharist was an incomplete
one, standing there unfulfilled, but brimming with hope for that
final fulfillment. That hope, that burning dream, is an essential
part of the black personality and black experience.

The people of the community, who gathered around the gospel that way in a growing acceptance of a black Christ, took on
a new appreciation of themselves. If Christ is black, then black
is indeed beautiful. The blacks in the community began seeing
themselves as important in the church, as necessary for the
church, as the only hope of renewal for the church, as the heart
of the revolution in organized Christianity for a refounding of
the church of Christ for our age.

To join their community was to join a people struggling for
freedom from oppression, persecution, meaninglessness. The
people of this gospel community started out with a very naive
and antiquated vision of the church and Christianity—a vision
passed on to them by those in charge of the church at that time,
a people running out of steam, a tired and jaded people with
nothing more to say about the Christ. But the people of the

gospel community (moved by the restless Spirit) have developed into a people with a kind of breakthrough theological vision surrounding their black Christ.

The lack of black Catholic clergy led the people to look for a new way to find ministers for their community. They asked the priest to contact the nearby university and the seminary to try to find teachers who would volunteer their time to provide brief and intense courses to those whom they would choose to be their ministers. Many teachers did volunteer and they set up courses that lasted about three months on subjects like Scripture, Church History, Liturgy, Vatican Council II, and Black Spirituality. Those who followed the courses came to be called Ministers of Service. They were not trained for a particular ministry but, rather, for any ministry that might develop out of the life of the community. One of them became a minister of the community's liturgy and grew into their preacher. Another became a minister to youth. A coach of a basketball team opened a ministry of sports. A professional musician chose to serve the music world. One of those trained was a politician, and he ventured into the world of politics with his Christian ministry. And they want their black priest, when they get one, to be trained within the black community—and presented to the bishop for ordination. The Ministers of Service are both men and women, and they are commissioned by the community itself.

The Bible community, which once could not see past its own problems, was led out into the deep. The catalyst was a pretty young biologist and mother who taught at the university. She came to the meetings of one of the groups with her husband and baby, mainly out of a deep-felt need to belong to some faith community. Her own faith, she confessed, was waning. She was not certain that she believed in anything beyond the Godhead itself, but she was deeply impressed by the unwavering faith of the community and was hoping some of it would rub off on her. One day during a particularly moving Eucharist, which had been preceded by an intense discussion of injustice in the world and in society and what had to be done about it, she spoke out. She mentioned how beautiful the Eucharist was, and how true and valid were their feelings on injustice and their planned actions to overcome it—but she wished she could convey her own con-

viction to them as powerfully as they had passed on theirs to
her. Her conviction was this: unless good people like this group
get into the struggle to preserve this world of ours from chemical
and nuclear poison and destruction, we shall reach that terrible
point where there will be no possibility of justice or injustice,
no possibility of Eucharist ever again. She was weeping openly
when she finished speaking, and the black militant Christian
community was silent.

The Bible study and reflection group, which had been transformed into a Basic Christian Community, began to get more
and more involved in the growing protest against nuclear war-
fare: in the beginning as a simple cry against the terrible drain-
ing-off of funds from the poor for the benefit of this monstrous
weaponry, but gradually their black voice was raised more
against the horror of it all.

Their voice was heard in other places too. In the chancery,
for instance. They had the audacity to seek an audience with
the bishop and then demand of him that the Catholic diocese
commit itself essentially, dramatically, and irrevocably to the
poor. What they were asking was that the diocese dig into its
sacred patrimony to procure the millions necessary to help provide the food, medicine, housing, and employment that the poor
needed, and to all of which they had a right. They were out of
line, of course, and terribly naive and uninformed about ecclesiastical procedure and the rights of lay people under canon law.
They were dismissed peremptorily. The bishop never really
trusted them after that, and was always a little afraid of them.

Then there was the city, which had been abandoned to them
by the whites. They realized it would be up to them to bring
peace to the city, much as it had been up to the Jews to bring
peace to the hated city of Babylon to which God had exiled
them. Through the prophet Jeremiah, the Jews in Babylon were
told by God to build houses, settle down, plant gardens, take
wives, have sons and daughters and increase, and to "work for
the good of the city to which I, Yahweh, have exiled you. Pray
on its behalf, for in its peace and Shalom, you will find your
peace" (Jer. 29:4–10).

The black Basic Community realized that, despite the monumental task facing it in the city, they would, as Christians, have

to act as leaven there. They would have to settle down in the city into which they had been brought in exile. They would have to work for the good of the city and pray for it, because in its peace they would find their peace.

As time went by, the parish church building, which at one time seemed so essential to them, became less and less important. They used it occasionally for the total gathering of the different gospel communities, with one or the other of the communities of the former parish leading the liturgy in the style it had developed back in the neighborhoods. But they did not have Sunday Mass there every week, because the peculiar rhythm of their lives, with its ups and downs, dictated against an automatically recurring Sunday Mass. The center of gravity of the church shifted from the parish buildings to the neighborhoods where the people lived and struggled. The style of the church could no longer be described as Neo-Gothic or Romanesque or Modern; it had the look and texture of their lifestyle—a strong community of believers in the midst of the fractured communities of the city. The finances no longer revolved around maintenance of buildings, but around the building of human community. They stopped counting the number of communions and confessions and parish members. The roster now included people of different faiths who had decided that if they were going to work together all week long fighting crime in their streets and homes, working for housing, the elderly, youth, and better health in their neighborhoods, they were not going to disperse and scatter to the four winds to pray somewhere else on Sundays.

The black Basic Community seemed hostile and even anti-white to outsiders, but it really was not. The people were still very welcoming. In effect, they were saying: "We are one with you—but change communities. Come, join the community of the oppressed, the poor, the lowly ones, those hungering and thirsting for food and justice, those who are crying now, those persecuted and abused and hated, those denounced as criminals—because the kingdom is theirs."

That was the gist and flavor of the letter they finally sent to the bishop one day:

Dear Bishop:

Peace. We send you our greetings from the Churches that meet in the houses of those who are truly black and authentically Catholic. Forgive us our weaknesses and sins. We forgive you. We are longing to see you, either to strengthen you by sharing our spiritual gifts with you, or, what is better, to find encouragement from you through our common faith. Greetings also to our fellow workers in Christ Jesus.

Be brave amidst the dangers of today. Stay firm in the faith. Be strong. Let everything you do be done in love. We pray for you, since we know that, in sharing our suffering, you will also share our consolation. Come visit us. We would be happy to break bread together with you, and we might celebrate the Lord's Supper that day, if you come.

If you visit the Vatican this year, please convey our filial love to the Bishop of Rome, and our greetings to the Church in Rome.

Shalom

Notes

1. YESTERDAY'S CHILDREN

1. Gary Wills, *Bare Ruined Choirs* (Garden City, N.Y.: Doubleday, 1971), pp. 15–37. Gary Wills captured, as well as anyone, the multifaceted spirit of the times, the all-embracing reality of growing up a Catholic before the time of Vatican Council II. It was a state of mind and attitude much easier to share than tò describe.

2. See Theodore Roszak, *Where the Wasteland Ends* (Garden City, N.Y.: Doubleday Anchor Books, 1973), pp. 103–4.

3. Ibid., pp. 114ff. The fundamentalist churches have taken up the crusade against idolatry, especially as they detect it in the Catholic church, an effort resulting in a virulent anti-Catholicism.

4. Pitirim Sorokin, *The Crisis of Our Age* (New York: E. P. Dutton, 1941), pp. 19–20.

5. Karl Rahner, "Towards a Fundamental Theological Interpretation of Vatican II,"*Theological Studies* 40, no. 47 (December 1979): 716–27.

6. The very positive steps toward ecumenism taken by Vatican Council II are absolutely necessary steps for the dream of a world church. Talk of a world church is only partially accurate as long as the Protestant-Catholic scandal endures. The present age and the future age will afford less time and even less credibility to a sectarian and divided church that is becoming more of a minority in the world with every passing day.

7. Rahner, "Towards a Fundamental Theological Interpretation," pp. 717ff.

8. Ibid., pp. 718–19.

9. Ibid., p. 721.

10. Eusebius, *Ecclesiastical History,* II.1.3, as quoted by Jean Daniélou in "Christianity as a Jewish Sect," *The Crucible of Christianity,* ed. Arnold Toynbee (New York: World Publishing Co., 1969), p. 262.

11. Daniélou, "Christianity as a Jewish Sect," p. 262.

157

12. Eusebius, *Ecclesiastical History,* III.32.5–6.

13. Daniélou, "Christianity as a Jewish Sect," p. 262. See Daniélou, *The Theology of Jewish Christianity* (London, 1964), for the only treatment of the doctrines and customs of Judeo-Christians in their entirety.

14. Daniélou, "Christianity as a Jewish Sect," p. 275.

15. Ibid., p. 276.

16. Oscar Cullmann, *Saint Pierre* (Paris, 1952), as quoted by Daniélou, "Christianity as a Jewish Sect," p. 276.

17. Daniélou, "Christianity as a Jewish Sect," p. 277; Samuel George Frederick Brandon, *The Fall of Jerusalem and the Christian Church* (London: SPCK, 1931), pp. 217–48; Hornschuh, *Studien zur Epistula Apostolorum* (Berlin, 1965), pp. 96–116.

18. Daniélou, "Christianity as a Jewish Sect," p. 262.

19. Raimundo Panikkar, *The Trinity and the Religious Experience of Man* (Maryknoll, N.Y.: Orbis Books, 1973), p. 58.

2. THE DYING OF AN AGE

1. Joseph Klausner, *Jesus of Nazareth,* p. 368, as quoted by H. Richard Niebuhr, *Christ and Culture* (New York: Harper Torchbooks, 1951), pp. 2ff.

2. Niebuhr, *Christ and Culture,* p. 3.

3. Klausner, as quoted in Niebuhr, *Christ and Culture,* p. 3.

4. Edward Schillebeeckx, *Ministry* (New York: Crossroad, 1981), p. 6.

5. Pitirim Sorokin, *The Crisis of Our Age* (New York: E. P. Dutton, 1941), pp. 21–22.

6. Ibid., p. 19.

7. Ibid., p. 20.

8. Ibid., pp. 35–36.

9. Niebuhr, *Christ and Culture,* pp. 42, 128ff. Niebuhr describes at length the genius of Thomas Aquinas: "Thomas Aquinas is probably the greatest of all the synthesists in Christian history. . . . In his system of thought he combines without confusing philosophy and theology, state and church, civic and Christian virtues, natural and divine laws, Christ and culture."

10. Sorokin, *The Crisis of Our Age,* p. 13.

11. William Blake, *The Complete Writings of William Blake* (New York: Oxford University Press, 1966). In Blake's view, Bacon and Newton had to be numbered among the great betrayers of the human spirit, with their insistence on the uniqueness of science as the only path to truth.

12. Richard Wolkomir, "The Dawning of Desertron," *American Way,* July 23, 1985.

13. Karl Rahner, "Towards a Fundamental Theological Interpretation of Vatican II," *Theological Studies* 40, no. 47 (December 1979), p. 725.

14. Sorokin, *The Crisis of Our Age,* p. 13.

15. Alvin Toffler, *The Third Wave* (New York: Bantam Books, 1980), pp. 9–10.

16. Ibid., p. 28.

17. Ibid., pp. 84–97.

18. Ibid., pp. 46–60.

3. THE CHURCH: CAPTIVE OF THE INDUSTRIAL REVOLUTION

1. Rahner, "Towards a Fundamental Theological Interpretation of Vatican II," *Theological Studies* 40, no. 47 (December 1979), p. 725.

2. Walbert Bühlmann, *The Coming of the Third Church* (Maryknoll, N.Y.: Orbis Books, 1977), pp. 13–24. Bühlmann gives the title *first church* to the Oriental church, possessing the rights of the first-born (the first eight councils were held on Eastern soil). The *second church* is the Western church. He sees the *third church* as that of the new nations now entering history, the church of the third world.

3. *New Catholic Encyclopedia* (New York: McGraw-Hill, 1976), vol. 1, pp. 305, 375; vol. 8, p. 913; vol. 10, p. 58; vol. 13, p. 905.

4. Ibid., vol. 3, pp. 369–74.

5. Ibid., vol. 3, pp. 248–49.

6. See Alvin Toffler, *The Third Wave* (New York: Bantam Books, 1980), p. 31. Government bureaucracies, hospitals, schools, and seminaries took on many of the characteristics of the factory—division of labor, hierarchical structure for the sake of the "products" turned out by the institution, school-grading policies, admission procedures, and accreditation were standardized and transferred to seminary training.

7. Some of the largest Catholic major seminaries in the world today are situated in Africa and South Korea.

8. Toffler, *Third Wave,* pp. 49–51.

9. See Leonardo Boff, "Ecclesia Docens vs. Ecclesia Discens," in *Church: Charism and Power* (New York: Crossroad, 1985), pp. 138ff.

10. See ibid., p. 123.

11. It was only in the nineteenth century that the Catholic Missions came under the direct control of the papacy, during the reign of Pope Gregory XVI, and they have remained so until the present time. Until then there was great disorder and confusion due to the local autonomy of missionary areas under the control of the different bishops of the

world who had sent out their own missionaries. So, in the interest of greater order, efficiency, and control, Pope Gregory reorganized the whole Catholic missionary endeavor and centralized it under Vatican auspices (see *New Catholic Encyclopedia,* vol. 6, p. 786).

12. Paul is merely following tradition, evident in the Gospels in such ideas as the Great Commission (Mt. 28:18–20) and the references in John concerning the power to forigve sins.

13. *A New Catechism: Catholic Faith for Adults* (New York: Herder and Herder, 1967), p. 225. The Gesu and St. Peter's in Rome are examples of the assembly-hall type of church.

4. THE MEDITERRANEAN CHIRST

1. Bruce Vawter, *The Man Jesus* (Garden City, N.Y.: Doubleday, 1973), p. 94.

2. Edward Schillebeeckx, *Jesus: An Experiment in Christology* (New York: Crossroad, 1979), p. 64.

3. Ibid., p. 65.

4. Raimundo Panikkar, *The Trinity and the Religious Experience of Man* (Maryknoll, N.Y.: Orbis Books, 1973), p. 58.

5. Schillebeeckx, *Jesus,* pp. 67–71.

6. Ibid., p. 66.

7. Ibid., p. 67.

8. Ibid., p. 68.

9. Ibid., p. 71.

10. Ibid., p. 72.

11. Ibid., p. 70.

12. See Gustavo Gutiérrez, *A Theology of Liberation* (Maryknoll, N.Y.: Orbis Books, 1973; rev. ed., 1988); Leonardo Boff, *Teologia do Cativeiro e da Libertação* (Petrópolis: Vozes, 1977); James H. Cone, *Black Theology and Black Power* (New York: Seabury Press, 1969); G. Clarke, "American Theology in Black: James H. Cone," *Cross Currents* 22, no. 2 (Spring 1972).

13. Thomas Sheehan, "The End of Catholicism: Revolution in Catholicism," *New York Review of Books,* June 14, 1984.

14. David Tracy, "Levels of Liberal Consensus," *Commonweal,* August 10, 1984, pp. 425–30.

15. Andrew M. Greeley, "The Ways of Knowing," *Commonweal,* August 10, 1984, pp. 431–35.

16. Ibid., p. 432.

5. SACRAMENTS FOR THE WORLD

1. What Aquinas says is not so extraordinary in the light of the New Testament itself. St. John speaks of the Word being present at the beginning (Jn. 1:3, 18) with all things visible and invisible coming to be through the Word. St. Paul is even more daring in speaking of the Incarnate Word, the Jesus of history, as being there at the beginning, the first-born of all creation, in whom all things are created, "in him, through him and for him," the created image of the unseen God (Col. 1:15; 1 Cor. 8:6; Heb. 1:3, 6; Eph. 1:10, 21). The eternal generation of the Word and the world of creation, made in, through, and for Jesus Christ, really result from the identical act of the ineffable and inscrutable will of God.

2. Karl Rahner, "How to Receive a Sacrament and Mean It," *The Sacraments: Readings in Contemporary Sacramental Theology,* ed. Michael J. Taylor (New York: Alba House, 1981), p. 74.

3. Ibid., pp. 74, 77.

4. Ibid., pp. 73–74.

5. Ibid., p. 74.

6. Ibid., p. 79.

7. Ibid., p. 75.

8. Joseph M. Powers, "Eucharist, Mystery of Faith and Love," *The Sacraments* (New York: Alba House, 1981), p. 119.

9. Vatican Council II, "The Constitution on the Sacred Liturgy," *The Conciliar and Post-Conciliar Documents,* ed. Austin Flannery (Collegeville, Minn.: Liturgical Press, 1975), pp. 4–5; Everett A. Diederich, "The Unfolding Presence of Christ in the Celebration of the Mass," *The Sacraments* (New York: Alba House, 1981), pp. 129ff.

10. Rahner, "How to Receive a Sacrament," pp. 74–75.

6. THE THIRTEENTH APOSTLE

1. The distinction between revelation and religion in this chapter follows the thought of the French theologian Jacques Ellul, and it underlines the necessity of not considering Christianity to be a religion.

2. Dietrich Bonhoeffer, *The Cost of Discipleship* (New York: Macmillan, 1963), pp. 77ff. Bonhoeffer stresses the personal element in the story of the rich young man, both the person of the young man and the person of the one whom he has been called to follow.

7. THE CHURCH OF THE THIRD WAVE

1. "The New Catechism? Here It Is!" *The Wanderer* 119, no. 2 (January 9, 1986): 1.

2. Ibid., p. 6.

3. William J. Bausch, *A New Look at the Sacraments* (Mystic, Conn.: Twenty-Third Publications, 1983), pp. 163–64. Cf. 1 Cor. 5:1–5; Tit. 3:10; 1 Tim. 3:10.

4. Ibid., p. 177.

5. Leonardo Boff, *Church: Charism and Power* (New York: Crossroad, 1985), pp. 50, 80, 81.

6. Ibid., p. 142.

7. Ibid.

8. Ibid., pp. 122–23.

9. Jerome Murphy-O'Connor, "House Churches and the Eucharist: Archeological Light from Paul's Corinth," *The Bible Today* 22, no. 1 (January 1984): 50.

8. HEIRS OF THE WORLD

1. Thomas Berry, "Creative Energy," *Riverdale Papers I* (from papers and lectures of the Riverdale Center for Religious Research, Riverdale, N.Y., 1978), pp. 1–2.

2. William Blake, as quoted by Theodore Roszak, *Where the Wasteland Ends* (Garden City, N.Y.: Doubleday Anchor Books, 1973), p. 99.

3. Pitirim Sorokin, *The Crisis of Our Age* (New York: E. P. Dutton, 1941), p. 19.

4. Berry, "Building the Earth," *Riverdale Papers I,* pp. 1, 9–10.

5. Berry, "Creative Energy," p. 5.

6. H. Richard Niebuhr, *Christ and Culture* (New York: Harper Torchbooks, 1951), pp. 7–8.

7. Raimundo Panikkar, *The Intra-Religious Dialogue* (New York: Paulist Press, 1978).

8. Berry, "Cosmic Person and the Future of Man," *Riverdale Papers II,* pp. 5–6.

9. Berry, "Building the Earth," p. 9; "Traditional Religions," *Riverdale Papers II,* p. 2.

10. Nalini Devdas, "The Theandrism of Raimundo Panikkar and Trinitarian Parallels in Modern Hindu Thought," *Journal of Ecumenical Studies* 17 (1980): 610.

11. Berry, "Threshold of the Modern World," *Riverdale Papers II,* p. 13.

12. Berry, "Religious Studies and the Global Community of Man," *Riverdale Papers II.* This entire chapter deals with the direction such a conversion might take.

13. Job, chaps. 38–39; Exod. 14:13–25; Ps. 74:12–15. The authors of the Bible delighted in projecting accounts of creation into the experience of redemption, hearing God in the tramping of victorious soldiers' feet in Jewish military battles. The American Indian does the same, seeing the sun, trees, and animals as places where God has "stopped."

14. Berry, "Cosmic Person and the Future of Man," p. 7; "The Dynamics of the Future," p. 1; "Planetary Management," *Riverdale Papers VI,* pp. 3, 12.

9. PREACHING THE GOSPEL TO AMERICA

1. America is chosen as an example of a culture to be evangelized, not because of arbitrary ethnocentricity, but because of its importance as a dominant force in the scientific-technological culture that is sweeping the globe.

2. Berry, "Cosmic Person and the Future of Man," *Riverdale Papers I,* p. 7.

3. Ibid.

4. Berry, "Building the Earth," *Riverdale Papers I,* p. 1.

5. Berry, "Cosmic Person and the Future of Man," pp. 3, 4.

6. Ibid., p. 6. Thomas Berry, S.J., might be called an English-speaking Teilhard de Chardin. But that comparison does not do him justice as a thinker in his own right, as a true theologian of ecology and creation.

Index